CW00643408

Seeing in the Dark

Christopher Chapman is Spiritual Formation Adviser for the Diocese of Southwark, having served as a priest in the Roman Catholic Church for nine years. He is a spiritual director and helps to train authorized lay workers in pastoral care ministry.

Seeing in the Dark

*Pastoral perspectives on suffering from
the Christian spiritual tradition*

Christopher Chapman

CANTERBURY
PRESS
Norwich

© Christopher Chapman 2013

This Edition published in 2013 by Canterbury Press
Editorial office
108-114 Golden Lane
London EC1Y 0TG

Canterbury Press is an imprint of Hymns Ancient and Modern Ltd
(a registered charity)
13a Hellesdon Park Road, Norwich, Norfolk, NR6 5DR

www.canterburypress.co.uk

All rights reserved. No part of this publication may be reproduced,
stored in a retrieval system, or transmitted,
in any form or by any means, electronic, mechanical,
photocopying or otherwise, without the prior permission of
the publisher, Canterbury Press.

Christopher Chapman has asserted his right under the Copyright,
Designs and Patents Act, 1988,
to be identified as the Author of this Work

British Library Cataloguing in Publication data

A catalogue record for this book is available from the British Library

978 1 84825 259 2

Typeset by Manila Typesetting Company
Printed and bound by
CPI Group (UK) Ltd, Croydon

Contents

This book is dedicated in memory of my parents,
Bridget and Peter.

Acknowledgements

Writing this book would have probably been impossible (and certainly more miserable!) without the support of my wife June and the encouragement of my family and friends. I am also grateful to the staff of the spirituality department of Heythrop College for the teaching that spurred this exploration, and to Canterbury Press for giving me this opportunity. Finally my thanks go to those who have so generously accompanied me on my halting journey through life and to those who have trusted me to guide them. I have learnt so much.

I am grateful for permission to use excerpts from the following works:

An Interrupted Life, The Diaries and Letters of Etty Hillesum 1941– 43, with a preface by Eva Hoffman and introduction by Jan C. Gaarlandt, translated from the Dutch by Arnold J. Pomerans, 1999, Persephone Books, 59 Lamb's Conduit Street, London WC1N 3NB

Hadewijch, The Complete Works, from The Classics of Western Spirituality Series, translation and introduction by Mother Columba Hart O.S.B., preface by Paul Monmaers. Copyright © Paulist Press inc. 1980, New York/Mahwah, N.J. Used with permission of Paulist Press. www.paulistpress.com

Julian of Norwich, Showings, from The Classics of Western Spirituality Series, translated and introduced by Edmund Colledge and James Walsh, preface by Jean Leclercq O.S.B. Copyright © Paulist Press inc. 1978, New York/Mahwah, N.J. Used with permission of Paulist Press. www.paulistpress.com

Prayers of life, Michael Quoist, 1965, Gill and Macmillan, Dublin. Published in North America as *Prayers* by Sheed and Ward, an imprint of Rowman and Littlefield Publishers Inc.

Revelations of Divine Love by Julian of Norwich, translated by Elizabeth Spearing, introduction and notes by A.C. Spearing (Penguin Classics, 1998). Translation copyright © Elizabeth Spearing, 1998. Introduction and Notes © A.C. Spearing, 1998. Reproduced by permission of Penguin Books Ltd.

Story of a Soul, translated by John Clarke, O.C.D. Copyright © 1975, 1976, 1996 by Washington Province of Discalced Carmelites ICS Publications, 2131 Lincoln Road, N.E. Washington, DC 20002-1199 U.S.A. www.icspublications.org

The Collected Works of St. John of the Cross, translated by Kieran Kavanaugh and Otilio Rodriguez. Copyright © 1964, 1979, 1991 by Washington Province of Discalced Carmelites ICS Publications, 2131 Lincoln Road, N.E. Washington, DC 20002-1199 U.S.A. www.icspublications.org

The Spiritual Exercises of St. Ignatius of Loyola translated by Louis J. Puhl S.J. (Newman Press 1951). Reprinted with permission from Loyola Press. To order copies of this book, call 1-800-621-1008, or visit www.loyolabooks.org

Waiting for God by Simone Weil, translated by Emma Craufurd, translation copyright 1951, renewed © 1979 by G.P. Putnam's Sons. Used by permission of G.P. Putnam's Sons, a division of Penguin Group (USA) Inc.

The Scripture quotations contained herein are from the New Revised Standard Version of the Bible, Anglicized Edition, copyright © 1989, 1995, by the Division of Christian Education of the National Council of the Churches of Christ in the United States of America and are used by permission. All rights reserved.

Introduction

Is it possible to see in the dark? In one sense the answer is 'no', for absence of light disables sight. But do we only see with our eyes? What about the vision that comes through imagination, intuition or hope? If I close my eyes my imagination can take me wherever I choose to be. Pay attention to the inmost stirrings of my spirit and intuition can look beneath the surface of events to sense the significance of what is taking place. Gaze through the window of hope and I am led from what is now to what will be. The fall of darkness invites new ways of seeing.

The night world of suffering disrupts familiar patterns of functioning. We find ourselves blundering in the dark; our normal responses and expectations no longer seem to work. But what if there were other ways of meeting this experience? If we could draw on them then we might not only survive but, against all the odds, begin to grow. We are not the first to struggle. There is wisdom to turn to, honed within the lives of those who also woke to difficult days and heavy hearts. This book explores what the Christian spiritual tradition across time and place has to say about how we respond to difficulty and pain, and where we encounter God within them. We are in the dark yet, with this help, we can begin to see.

We all struggle

How are we to respond to suffering? All of us face the question, for however hard we try we cannot navigate our way around it. Thankfully it is not the only reality and I for one gladly welcome

laughter and joy. But even so, our struggles are more than inter-
ference on the radio, solved by the turning of a dial. Suffering simply 'is'. Our vocabulary tells the same story; we put names on our
pain: sorrow, anguish, disappointment, rejection, frustration . . .
the list goes on. Take time to consider any one of these headings and
most of us can bring events, past or present, to mind.

We recognize too that our pain has different layers: if we suffer physically for a length of time or with any regularity then the
experience is likely to affect us emotionally and we might feel low
or disappointed or fearful of the future. Sometimes there is a flow
back in the opposite direction: worry too much and you invite a
headache; the toll of prolonged mental stress can express itself in
a weakened immune system. Inward struggle has an impact on
our external relationships. There are times when the intensity or
persistence of our emotional pain makes it almost impossible to
conduct 'normal' conversation; we feel wholly absorbed by what
is taking place within and isolated from others who live in such a
very different world. And it is when we hurt most that spiritual
questions rise to the surface: 'Why is this happening to me? Why
doesn't God do something? What have I done to deserve this?'

Some pain can be traced back to our own actions. When we
realize we have let down those we care for most, it is a torment
to look ourselves in the eye. But even the good we desire can have
its difficult downside. There is more than one story of lottery win-
ners failing to adjust to the wealth they once longed for and falling apart under the pressures their 'good fortune' created. Other
suffering visits us unexpectedly, wholly outside our control: illness, redundancy, or the collapse of a relationship we built our
existence around. Then there is the hard work of bearing our own
anxieties and insecurities. We are often our own most difficult
neighbour: 'When, O when will I be delivered from me?'

Looking back I suspect we can see positive things that have come
from difficult experiences: a deeper level of self-understanding or the
discovery of inner resources we were hitherto unaware of. Times of
struggle can give us a keener awareness of the giftedness of what we
have taken for granted, and may enhance our ability to come alongside another with compassion. Suffering asks questions of us; it has

the capacity to disturb us out of a half-awake existence and to impel us to live for what we sense matters. But suffering can also stunt growth, leading us to live narrowly and fearfully. Our spirit, self-esteem, spark can be dimmed and diminished as easily as stirred into life. I can see both taking place within my own story. What makes the difference? Is it the extent of our pain or our response to it?

For those brought up to believe in a God of love revealed in the person of Christ, our struggles and suffering bring further questions: 'Why does a compassionate God allow this to happen? Why doesn't he do something to take this hurt away?' There is a puzzle at the heart of the Jesus story: a God who as creator and lord is limitless in power, expressed in the powerlessness of a crucified man; a presence in our pain – yes – but not an answer to it.

More questions than answers

It is within lesser pains as well as greater that our questions arise. Some years back I applied for a post in a charitable organization. I spent hours filling in a detailed application form and then went through two rounds of interviews, preparing and making two separate presentations. A polite letter of rejection followed. Then a second post came up with the same organization, and whereas the first had been one I felt I could stretch myself to, this one seemed tailor-made. I filled in the application form, went through two more rounds of interviews with two more presentations. All seemed to go well, but another 'no, but we wish you every success in the future' fell on the doormat. A well-meaning friend sought to comfort me: 'It was obviously not meant to be; there is something better waiting for you.' Perhaps there was, but if so why put me through all that? And how far could I really believe that my interviewers were active agents of God making sure I didn't make the wrong move? Though I threw my frustration at God I realized that responsibility did not belong at his door. The experience simply and uncomfortably 'was', and what mattered now was the nature of my response. How was I going to weave this happening into my story in such a way that it moved me towards life rather than disintegration, and how was God going to be there for me as I sought this? Whether or not we can find an explanation for the course of events that satisfies us – and often this is beyond us – we have to find a way of responding that makes some meaning within how things are. So along with the inevitable 'why?' there are other questions that become important:

- By what process do we 'grow up', humanly and spiritually? Is suffering a necessary part of this process? If so, how and why?
- Given that we do feel pain, how are we to meet it?
- What might be the fruit of suffering, and how do we enable this fruit to grow?
- Where is God when we suffer?
- Does suffering distance us or unite us to God?
- What is the significance of the suffering of the Son of God for our own experience of pain and struggle?
- Is the very experience of God a source of our discomfort as well as our joy? And if so, why?

These are not abstract questions; they flow from life. They express a search for meaning amidst events that can seem entirely random and meaningless. On this journey I have found some light for my path through the lives and writings of people from the past. Their witness and wisdom have enabled me to sense God's intimate presence and leading amidst my disorientation. If they have not always provided me with answers, they have at least guided me to ask the right questions, and so move forward in hope of their resolution.

A cloud of witnesses

Therefore, since we are surrounded by so great a cloud of witnesses, let us also lay aside every weight and the sin that clings so closely, and let us run with perseverance the race that is set before us. (Hebrews 12.1)

Why look to people from the past, living in contexts often far removed from our own, to find answers to our own questions? Perhaps we might do so because truth is elusive, and our understanding is partial at best. We need all the help we can get. We have a notion of progress: that each succeeding generation is better equipped, more informed, and therefore knows more about the realities of the universe than those that have gone before. In some areas this assumption seems to stand up. We know more about the motions of the stars and planets and the process by which life evolved from its beginnings than anyone living just a few centuries ago. And if we are a little hazy about the facts we can always go on the internet. But do we really know anything more about love, or how to be whole, or the way to face death?

These truths that matter so deeply to us are not so easily bottled. No one has just our experience and ultimately no one else has to face the challenge of making some sense of it. We do not need some universal and definitive explanation; it will not fit our very particular reality. But we do need some companions willing to share their understanding with us: witnesses whose testimony rhymes in some way with our own. They provide us with a map that, whilst not exact, gives us confidence to begin to judge where we have come from and where we might go to. They put into words what we have not yet been able to frame in speech. The people whose witness I call upon in this book are just such companions for me. Some live in times whose spirit feels not so very different from our own. Others come from further away, but the very difference of time, culture and means of expression casts a fresh light for our tired eyes: a new way of seeing things foreign to our familiar surroundings – like seeing my back garden in a way I have never done before from a neighbour's window. Often they used word pictures – metaphors – to describe what happens for us within a time of struggle, and how we might co-operate with the work of God within the experience. The same images recur, now played this way and now that. As our imagination enters the picture we begin to re-view what is taking place and reconsider how we might respond.

With John of the Cross we will explore the imagery of darkness and night. Where is God when we cannot see our way? Night carries with it a sense of threat, confusion and isolation. And yet there are some things we see and understand in the dark that are not available to us in daylight. Night invites our trust in the hidden presence of God. Relationship unexpectedly deepens.

In the Old Testament we read of the struggle of Jacob with an unknown stranger during the crossing of a river. Neither party will give way. Jacob eventually emerges limping, but with the gift of a blessing and a new name. He recognizes he has wrestled with God and that his life will never be the same. George Herbert, Gerard Manley Hopkins and Hadewijch used poetry to express their own conflicts with God. In their words we might find expressed our questions, complaints and doubts. What will the fruit of this struggle be for us?

Hadewijch saw her life played out in the rhythm of the seasons. Within the turning year there are times of renewal and of ending. There are long months of dormancy when no life seems visibly to stir; yet look harder and the hazel blooms in mid-winter. What season are we now experiencing? How can we move in step with the time rather than fight against it?

The biblical story of the Fall explores how humankind lost its original happiness and balance. Destructiveness entered into human relationships and life became a struggle for survival. Julian of Norwich retells the story of the Fall in her attempt to reconcile how a loving God can allow his creation to suffer. She sees how God enters into the pain of his loved ones. She saw that in the end we can only fall as far as Christ, who willingly descends into our hurt and confusion.

In his hymn *Guide me O thou great Jehovah*, the Welsh Methodist preacher William Williams compares our anxious progress through difficult and challenging experiences with the wanderings of the Israelites through the wilderness. Between slavery in Egypt and the Promised Land of milk and honey lies a trackless wasteland without path or way. We too are sometimes caught in an in-between place, unsure of where the road to life goes or whether it is possible to find lost meaning. Yet we do not travel alone and, though the destination remains obscure, the journey itself begins to form us.

Sometimes our pain stems from a distorted understanding of who we are, where happiness lies and how we move towards it. We inherit or learn ways of seeing and behaving that are self-defeating and limiting. *The Spiritual Exercises* of Ignatius of Loyola suggest ways we can recognize these unhealthy patterns of thought and action, and move with the Spirit towards our wholeness and freedom.

Within the growth of relationship we experience both times of intense meeting and times of distance and separation. With God, intimately with us and yet always out of reach, the ebb and flow of felt absence and presence is painfully unsettling. Yet, as the philosopher and spiritual seeker Simone Weil explained, meeting and separation are two sides of one reality: the formation of an unbreakable bond of belonging and mutual commitment.

Finally I will explore what fruit might be gathered from the tree of the cross of our struggles and Christ's Passion. Fruit takes its own time to mature. Some we can reach and take from the branches, whilst other fruits only become available when at last they ripen and fall to the ground. We meet Etty Hillesum who found amidst suffering the personal integration she longed for.

Each chapter sets out to have integrity within its limits, and some will speak more to the place you find yourself than others. So it may be this is a book you can read in stages, pondering the imagery that is presented and seeing where it connects with your experience. On the other hand the different metaphors complement one another. No one image by itself can wholly unravel what in the end remains mysterious. There are truths that are only understood in living through them, and even then they elude being neatly wrapped up in words of explanation. But, put together, the imagery builds up a fuller picture of how we might meet suffering when it comes our way, and respond to the work of a creative, resourceful and compassionate God within it.

This book is written for those who experience suffering and difficulty, and those who seek to support them as spiritual directors, pastoral care workers or Christian ministers. The two groups are not as different from each other as might first appear. Those involved in supporting others also have to deal with their own challenges. And those who now suffer may find fruit within the experience that in turn they can share with others. We are all helpers and all the helped. Nevertheless I will include some pointers for those who accompany others through the difficult and painful. These will largely focus on the spiritual questions that arise and the nature of the support that might prove most useful.

I hope you will be moved to read more of the work of this cloud of witnesses. This book can do no more than provide the smallest of introductions. A brief biographical guide and the notes after each chapter point the way for you to delve more deeply.

I

Starting Points

We all start somewhere in terms of our interpretation of the significance of our struggles. As I grew up in a Catholic world in the 1960s, God and suffering seemed inevitably aligned. Everywhere about me Christ hung on the cross. The walls of the church plotted the stations of his journey towards death. At primary school I was fed stories of the martyrs who won eternal life through enduring the cruelty of others; and since their passage to heaven was so instant and guaranteed I naturally aspired to join them. God was a larger version of our teachers, rewarding good behaviour in the next life, if not in this, and punishing wrongdoing. Life was a serious business, strewn with 'oughts' and 'shoulds' and most definitely not fun. And so I came to my own childhood theology based on a series of unacknowledged assumptions:

- 'Love' was dependent on the performance of good works.
- Wrongdoing must be paid for through repentance and pain.
- Christ suffered and died because of my/our sinfulness.
- The way to God is characterized by self-forgetfulness, expressed in sacrificing one's own happiness and enduring hardship.

My underlying suspicion was that the more miserable I was the better God was pleased! Yet the same tradition presented to me a compassionate Christ who sat with sinners and made them welcome. He was so moved by people's pain that he reached out to touch them and make them whole. He noticed the one at the back of the crowd who felt he was nothing and nobody. Might he also notice me? And so on the one hand I believed God wanted me to suffer, but on the other I glimpsed God with me in the mess I often felt my life to be.

Clearing the ground

Some years ago I began working an allotment. The plot had not been touched for years and all the most prolific and indomitable weeds had meanwhile come out to play: bindweed, couch grass, nettles, and brambles – a *Who's Who* of gardening nightmares. Before I could even think of growing anything, these had to be dug out. I sense something of the same in setting out to explore how we meet the experiences that most trouble and challenge us. Over the years I have been in receipt of many theories and beliefs about the nature of God and the significance of suffering. As often as not these strangled my attempts to integrate difficulties into my story in any way that felt healthy or life-giving. Instead I became stuck in resentment and despair, separated from a God I could not bring myself to trust. In accompanying others I have often glimpsed something similar taking place. As I listen to one person I feel the oppressive weight of a slave-driving God who lurks in the corners of their consciousness. In another I sense the enduring corrosive impact of teaching they received as a child. In reflecting on my own story and on hearing others, I recognize the ways in which negative personal experience warps perspective. Until these smothering weeds are identified and removed, seeds of understanding and meaning have little opportunity to germinate. I will begin then, with some weeding of the beliefs and attitudes that I sense get in the way of the growth of new shoots of perception.

Suffering is God-given punishment for sin

A familiar tale from the upbringing of many of us is that good deeds gain a reward and bad deeds a punishment. We are praised or criticized, treated or denied according to our actions. If this is so with human parents should it not also be true of God? And therefore – since God is the creator and maker of all – if we suffer, might it be because of the evil we have done that deserves punishment? The logic seems clear. But then experience tells us that the kind and generous are not excused hardship, whilst those who think only of themselves often thrive without any visible harm coming their way.

Almost at the physical centre of the Bible is the story of Job, a truly innocent man who nevertheless endures terrible suffering. His companions advise him to confess his sins to God and so find forgiveness and blessing, but Job insists he has done no wrong – and indeed he has not. Job's friends are only expressing the conventional wisdom of the time. But the author of Job wants to question the assumption that there is any easy correlation between the nature of our actions and divine blessing or curse. In Job's case, and in so many others, it simply does not match what happens. Even so, when life hurts we often cry out to God in anger and bewilderment, wondering what we have done to deserve this; and at a low point we may turn against ourselves, finding reason for misfortune in our own flawed nature. Job vents his anger and confusion at God who seems to set out to 'destroy both the blameless and the wicked'.[1] Such instincts run deep; we need something or someone to blame.

Perhaps we have a very human need to simplify: to say, 'if I do this, you will do that'. It might not be very comforting to think of God as one who imposes suffering as punishment but at least then we know where we are. But it won't wash: there are too many good people having a bad time and too many self-centred people prospering. In the end Job lets go of his charge against God, acknowledging his inability to know the deep working of the one who made and sustains the universe. It is unsurprising that we trace back the source of our pain to 'almighty God', interpreting our experience as some form of punishment; but in the long run such a belief will paralyse any attempt we make to grow through the challenges we face. The facts do not fit, and God is not an exaggeration of the worst of human failings.

---

1 Job 9.22

There are ways in which we may bring unhappiness on ourselves by not being centred in God and thereby being distanced from our true selves. In this sense we can say that 'sin' – this estrangement from God and our true nature – brings suffering. But it is too simple to say that therefore all suffering is God-given punishment for sin; suffering may sometimes be the *consequence* of our actions but is not *punishment*. The parable of the two sons explores these themes.[2] One son does the foolish thing: misspends his inheritance on wine, women and song, and gets himself in a terrible mess. He sets off for home having decided his father will not accept him as a son any more but he might as a servant; and even that humiliation would be better than his current self-induced misery. The other son stays at home and keeps his head down working, trusting that by doing so his father will favour him. To the upset of both, the father throws a party when his missing son returns, welcoming him back to the heart of the family. The consequence of the wayward son's actions would have been visible in his bedraggled clothes and drawn features; the 'punishment' he received was being treated like a king. The 'reward' for the son who stayed at home was the bitter pill of seeing the resources he had worked for now being spent on his wastrel brother, even though his father assured him: 'You are always with me and all that is mine is yours.' We might well scratch our heads at such a conclusion and such a God. Whatever we now endure is neither punishment nor reward. God uses a different and unfamiliar currency.

God brings about suffering so that we can grow

When we look back we may well see how fruitful a time of difficulty was for our personal development. We recognize that had life been entirely smooth and without challenge, we would never have made the same journey of self-discovery, nor been surprised by qualities hidden from us up until that point. Working with volunteers involved in pastoral care work, I am struck by the way their

---

2 Luke 15

passion for people's wellbeing and their ability to come along-side the vulnerable so often has its source in their own struggles. However, I question whether God actively sets out to make us suffer, even for a good end. Rather than this I think of suffering as part of the warp and weft of life. The rain falls and the sun shines: we have to meet life as it is. But God is in us and for us as we do so.

'There is nothing', St. Paul declares, 'that can separate us from the love of Christ' – no hardship, distress, persecution, not even death itself. In all things Christ is for us, and so 'all things work together for good'.[3] It is possible not only to survive suffering but to grow through it, and I believe God is alongside and within us as a motive force enabling this to happen. Yet God is not pull-ing the strings of day-to-day life, arranging that we meet suitable obstacles so that we attain a desired level of achievement.

Suffering is a good in itself, and so something to seek out

Christians have long understood the suffering of Christ to be redemptive: his pain heals our pain. The Song of the Servant in Isaiah 53 is used in the prayers and services of Holy Week to express the mystery of wholeness received through his self-gift:

> He was despised and rejected by others; a man of suffering and acquainted with infirmity . . . Surely he has borne our infirmities and carried our diseases . . . he was wounded for our transgres-sions, crushed for our iniquities; upon him was the punishment that made us whole, and by his bruises we are healed.[4]

If suffering transforms lives in such a way, should not those who follow Christ actively seek it out? A theme from my child-hood was that the pain that came our way should be 'offered up' in union with Christ for the salvation of the world. If we choose to suffer more, will not more blessing be released for the good of

3 Romans 8.28–39
4 Isaiah 53.3–5

others? However, before we go too far down this road, it is important to recognize that Christ never sought suffering as a good in
itself. He understood that continuing along the path he had
chosen of announcing the Good News of the Kingdom brought
him into conflict with religious and political authorities. He
saw – and he feared – the persecution that would come as a
consequence of his actions. But his choice was always to do
what was right and true rather than to seek suffering as an end
in itself. Suffering can bring the good, but it is never in itself
the good to be sought. Conscious avoidance of difficulty stunts
growth and closes us to the vulnerability involved in relationships based on trust. Those who go to every length to escape
pain will lead a shallow half-life. However, we do not need to
make our own trouble; it finds us within the natural course of
events. How we, meet it is important, but it is not for us to go
looking to make ourselves feel bad. God does not desire our
suffering and is not pleased with our misery, even if at times,
this is what we might feel!

Suffering is a way of subjugating the sinful, non-spiritual body

In this view the physical body and its desires are seen as sinful,
imprisoning our non-physical, spiritual selves. So we must punish or
subdue the body in order to find spiritual liberation. There is some
truth mixed in here: we do make our centre in the wrong things –
in having comfort, or power, or the good opinion of others – and so
must move beyond our immediate desires if we are to be centred in
God, in truth, and in love. This process is difficult, and often painful. Jesus endured 40 days of fasting in the wilderness at the very
beginning of his ministry. He came face to face with the physical and
emotional needs he must transcend if he was to express the depths
of his inner being in a way that was life-giving to others. I know that
if I am going to express love for another I will have to acknowledge,
yet go beyond, whatever draws me to pay sole attention to my need
for security or comfort or convenience. But the goal of the spiritual
journey is not to liberate the spirit from the body but to journey to a

renewed human life, as a whole and integrated person, in union with Christ who is body and spirit.

When I took up running in an effort to keep fit, my body soon told me to stop: 'You haven't enough oxygen and your legs are too weary.' My physical reactions were doing no more than seeking to protect me; their instincts needed to be heard. Yet I chose to go beyond what felt comfortable because I believed that my body had greater capacity than it protested to have on that day. With practice I found I could run at an even pace and not become breathless, and experience my legs as willing and able to go on beyond the first hundred yards. To go and run each day was not a way of beating the body up as worthless and lazy; instead it was a way of treating my body with honour and seeking to achieve its natural capacity. The body is also God's creation and we have no spiritual mode of being that is not rooted in our physicality. So 'no' to hair shirts, self-flagellation or any modern variation on the theme, but 'yes' to that discomfort that comes as we seek to liberate the potential of our God-given bodies.

Suffering is a departure from the normal

Culturally we have moved to a place where health, youth, vitality, success, and the ability to have control over our circumstances are projected as not just desirable but somehow 'normal', ignoring the fact that we do get unwell, grow older, meet failure and often experience a sense of powerlessness. Think for a moment of adverts for slimming products: why is everyone so unattainably thin? Why do promotional videos for new cars show them accelerating effortlessly along deserted mountain roads and not stuck in traffic on the M25? In an age when humankind is reputed to be able to control so much, pain has become seen as 'interruption' – a departure from the script. Because of this when we do suffer we feel more isolated – as if we have fallen off the map of how life is supposed to be. But now and then we do get stuck in traffic; events do not always turn out the way we would wish; most of us at one time or other will trip up on an uneven pavement and come crashing to the ground; and it will hurt. It is how human life is.

We are victims of fate. God's will is unalterable and fixed

There is not a fixed blueprint for each person's life: a single route to be taken, intended by God and ultimately unavoidable. We do, at least, have some measure of freedom. We have choices that are real and that shape our destiny. Nor does God manipulate events minutely according to some predetermined plan, so removing function and meaning from our responses. Yet in the face of someone's suffering or death I have heard it said more than once: 'We must accept it as God's will.' Perhaps what is being expressed is a sense of powerlessness over what is taking place. There comes a time too, when acceptance of the reality of 'what is' enables a more positive and meaningful response than the refusal to face things as they truly are. But God is not actively making the cancer grow, and does not engineer the car accident that so changes someone's life. God allows what takes place and does not or cannot alter the course of events. This raises questions enough that will run through the chapters that follow; but for now I want to resist the notion that God has already determined what will be, and that the fates are fixed against us.

Some starting points

Having identified some of the beliefs that I sense can get in the way of responding creatively to the difficulties we face, I want to suggest some lines of thinking to put in their place. These are themes that will be returned to and enlarged as we travel through this book. But it might help to introduce them here, so that you can greet them when they emerge once more and revisit the questions they will in themselves awake.

Suffering is a natural part of the rhythm of life

Rather than begin with the assumption that life should be easy, we embrace the reality that it is often difficult. Instead of believing that 'good' behaviour deserves reward, we accept that 'good' and 'bad' people experience difficulty in equal measure. At a rational level we might make such leaps; but then how often are we entirely rational? We are likely to find ourselves complaining bitterly that 'life is not fair', and, 'this shouldn't be happening' over trivial inconveniences as much as major life events. But at least we have a marker point to go back to that reflects facts rather than denies them. We can move forward, rather than be trapped in our indignant refusal to deal with the real.

We experience growing pains

We learn to walk by falling over. Gradually we discover how to balance ourselves and find a rhythm of movement that is consistent and stable – but not without some bumps. Most growth involves some pain as we extend ourselves beyond what has been hitherto familiar and comfortable. Spiritual development is not easy; sometimes it hurts. We are challenged to grow into a new way of relating. Rather than grabbing what we want, manipulating life and other people to suit us, God leads us into the ways of love. Love delivers us from seeing everything and everyone as an 'it' that has value only in so far as it meets our needs. Such limited perspective prevents us seeing and responding to what is before us as it really is. We have no eye for beauty or for wonder. Love lets go and lets be; it is open to give and receive freely and generously. Growing up into love enlarges our experience and is ultimately liberating and healing. But it is difficult and the process will sometimes upset us. We have to unlearn engrained attitudes. We must take the risk of trust if our relationships are going to deepen and become genuinely mutual. Along the way we are likely to find ourselves protesting that it hurts too much and we cannot go on.

A perspective on God's will

I have wrestled for some time with what is understood by 'God's will'. I realize that though 'doing God's will' is central to Christian discipleship, the phrase itself has dark shadows that can make its use uncomfortable. As I have already alluded, sometimes 'God's will' becomes shorthand for a belief in the implacable working of fate before which we can do nothing, usually in the context of events that are deeply troubling and painful. So much rests on our perception of who this God is whose will we invoke, and how this God is active within our experience. To pray 'your will be done' can be threatening or comforting, depending on our understanding. My understanding of 'God's will' is framed by the holding together of two thoughts. The first is that God loves us by letting go, and the second, that God loves us by becoming engaged in our story.

God loves us by not taking control of our lives. This is the humility of God. In freely choosing to create us, God creates us free. We are like God in this: that we can make what we will with what we have and who we are. We have real choices and God honours our choices. Rather than exercise control over us, God gifts us responsibility. Parents know that ultimately their children can only find selfhood by walking away and finding their own paths. We love not just by taking hold but by letting go. From making decisions for our children we move to giving our children the confidence to make their own choices and so discover and express their individuality. This same humility of God is exercised in relation to all that is created. God loves by creating and letting go. This is the incredible risk of God. God releases control, makes free. The result is that injustice and destructiveness persist, but also that generosity, creativity and love have the opportunity to flower. Being dealt with in this way can be uncomfortable for us. We have to do something more than letting events take their course. We are called to make choices, and as we do so we shape our own lives and those of people around us. We can build up or knock down, destroy or create, bring together or divide, share or withhold. Even when events seem to take us beyond anything we might have wanted or planned, we still have the power to decide how we will respond; and this choice is no less significant.

On the other hand, God loves us by becoming engaged in our story. When we pray 'your will be done' we are not letting go to an anonymous fate but choosing to align ourselves with God's active desire for his loved creation, expressed in the work of Jesus and the Spirit. Even as God lets go, God chooses to come alongside, not to compel us to obey, but to invite and enable us to choose life. The Christian tradition affirms the birth, life and death of Christ as the place where God vulnerably and generously embraces life as it is, with its messy mix of joy and pain, and by so doing transforms it. The event of Christ is not an answer, at least not in the sense of a statement that makes sense of all that seems to lack meaning in life and in death. Instead Jesus lives with our questions. He endures our limitations and experiences our defeats. In him we see God and humanity together traverse this unknowing darkness, not through explanation but by the simple act of living it. Where we are becomes a God-filled space.

God 'is' within the place where we are, and the place where we are is always the place where God begins from. The Bible as a whole tells this story; it is not an account of unbroken growth and the development of one clear, unalterable path; it is the story of God being found amongst the debris and confusion of missed opportunities and broken promises. In this story and our story we can glimpse God's heart's desire, not as unalterable fate taking control of our lives but as enduring and resourceful love that copes with whatever we choose to do and whatever happens to us along the way. Bad things still happen in God's world – incomprehensible things. Freedom leads to what is ugly as well as what is beautiful. God's desire is at work in Jesus, and in us if we choose it, through the Spirit, to make the ugly beautiful and build a kingdom here on earth that reflects that of heaven. We can use all our individuality and creativity in doing so; there is no pre-set plan. But there is the life-giving Spirit at work within our spirit to make all things new.

The place of mystery in our lives

In looking to understand suffering within our experience we are likely to experience a sense of mystery. Mystery might seem like a medieval hangover – a way of ducking or silencing difficult questions. I can still hear my primary school teacher deflecting potential objections from her class about how God could be three *and* one: 'It's no use looking for an answer, it is a mystery.' There are, after all, a great number of natural processes once mysterious that we can now explain: why the sun's light is temporarily eclipsed or why elements differ in their qualities. If the experience and impact of pain were reducible to concise and unambiguous explanation a book like this might be able to give clear answers and formulas: 'This is why it happened . . . this is what you must do . . . this will be the result.' But what we know when we are really hurting is that such definitive answers do not work: they afflict us with their certainty. Our experience just isn't that clear or that unambiguous. That is not to say we do not seek some purchase on what is happening and for what cause; or that wisdom gathered from experience is not helpful in knowing how to respond. But we cannot contain this event in mere sentences; it will always go beyond the words we use. We can journey towards what is true here but our understanding is always provisional; we never 'arrive'. Mystery, then, is about confronting a reality that we can begin to unravel and respond to, but one that we cannot wholly comprehend or control. Sometimes this experience awakens our wonder and joy, for beauty is also 'mysterious'. But the difficulty of letting go into mystery is also one of the roots of our pain.

The birth of a child, the death of one we have loved, the lifelong process of self-discovery with its many surprises, all have this sense of mystery. So too does our journey in God. God is always more and beyond; knowable yet ungraspable. There is much to say, but always more that remains unspoken for lack of knowledge and for the absence of words that work.

The place of paradox

The Gospels are full of paradox: life is gained through death, lordship is shown in service, the last shall be first, we give to receive, the humble are exalted, and the power of God is shown in weakness.

We will meet further paradox as we travel through these pages; for example we shall see that the Christian spiritual tradition affirms God both as light *and* darkness, and that the path to finding self often leads through a wilderness where everything tells us we are profoundly lost! Paradox reflects mystery within our experience; the deepest truths cannot be told in straight lines. Opposites that ordinarily have no place with each other make home together in uneasy coalition, edging us closer towards truths that remain ultimately inexpressible.

Paradox points us beyond the obvious and familiar to truths arrived at only through living them. When my father died I felt bereft and full; as close to him in his absence as I had ever experienced in life. Such experiences leave us wondering, aware that our conventional ways of perceiving are being overturned. This is why poetry and visual imagery figure so greatly within the Bible and spiritual writing across time. A line from a poem or a picture we gaze at halts us in our rush for instant understanding. And then, in the midst of what seems to make no sense, we glimpse meaning.

Meeting life as it is

How do we deal with life as it is?

- When events happen in a random way and caring people suffer whilst those who only think of themselves thrive.
- Where God doesn't always intervene and put things right in the way we hope.
- Where we meet disappointment, rejection and injustice.
- Where we get ill, and grow older, and all must die.

The answer for most of us is: 'with difficulty!' Yet the Christian Gospel is all about difficulty. Its symbol is a cross on which Jesus experienced a criminal's death in lonely desolation. Its message is that life dwells here. We might wish at times for some other life that is amenable, predictable and entirely pain free; or at the very least for a reliable anaesthetic to deliver us from its worst moments. But that would be some other life, not the one that you and I inhabit, nor the one where this compassionate and vulnerable God labours for our wholeness and our joy.

Now we will begin to explore the different ways the Christian spiritual tradition understands the place of suffering within our human and spiritual growth. What follows are not the cool, analytic theories of armchair theologians, safely removed from the firing line of daily difficulty. They derive from people who themselves struggled, not least in their relationship with God. They shared their perceptions generously, in the hope of making our passage easier than theirs sometimes was. We begin by plunging into the darkness of night and discovering what we might see there.

For reflection:

1] What are your own starting points for understanding the significance of struggle and difficulty, and the place of God within these experiences? How has any teaching or personal experience shaped your perspective?

2] Think back on a time when you experienced life as difficult. What did you learn about yourself? What questions arose within you during this period? What was your perception of where God was within this experience? Was God above you, alongside you, absent from you, within you, supporting you, neglecting you? How do you see this now?

2

In Darkness and Secure

One of my childhood memories is growing up in an all-electric house and regularly being plunged into darkness, announced by the cry: 'the shilling's gone'. A shilling wouldn't buy a lot of electricity now but then it was what stood between us and the night. After much desperate fumbling in pockets and the occasional collision with an unseen object, a shilling would be found and put in the meter; light was restored.

Whilst this sudden immersion into darkness and the confusion that followed was temporary and, by and large, fun, night-time for me was also about nightmares, threatening shadows and sleeplessness. I see myself: a small boy wandering downstairs, seeking the comfort of his parents' presence and of light; and I can sense my parents' weary exasperation as they tell me to 'lie back down and you'll soon go to sleep'. Still awake I would peer into the darkest corner of my room, convinced I could make out the shape of a gorilla hiding in its depths – not the greatest inducement to sleep! From the eerie glow of the street lamp outside, the shadows of wind-blown tree branches would sweep across the room like tentacles of terror. Night, however, held the gift of stars. I learnt the shape of constellations and, with a little telescope, saw double stars and red giants; and on the darkest nights of all – as far as I could get from the lights of houses and streetlamps – the cloudy haze of the Milky Way. Wonders ever-present but hidden; only revealed in darkness.

The imagery of night runs deep within our collective human memory, entering into our everyday language. When we are confused about the course of events we speak of 'being in the dark', and when understanding comes we 'see the light'. A person whose wisdom and clarity of thinking is to be admired is 'enlightened', but 'dark thoughts' are negative and destructive. Night expresses confusion: the inability to understand or come to terms with what is going on. We lose our way in darkness; our familiar landmarks are gone. We cannot find what we are looking for and life is no longer in our control. We may feel unsafe, threatened by unseen predators. We sense power is passing out of our hands, and that is deeply uncomfortable. At times like these, things 'look black'.

The Bible too has little good to say about the night. The uncreated world was 'a formless void' where 'darkness covered the face of the deep'. God called forth light from darkness and saw that 'the light was good'; but neglected to so affirm the darkness.[1] In John's Gospel, daylight expresses the life of God and darkness its absence. Jesus declares: 'I am the light of the world: anyone who follows me will not be walking in the dark, but will have the light of life.'[2] John marks the destructive impact of Judas' betrayal of Jesus with the simple, stark observation: 'It was night.'[3]

The first 'Christian' book I ever read, apart from the Bible, was *Prayers of Life* by the French priest, Michel Quoist. I found there many thoughtful and uplifting reflections and prayers that helped put shape on my own experience of God. And amongst them this troubled cry of anguish:

> Lord it is dark.
> Lord, are you here in my darkness?
> Your light has gone out and so has its reflection on people and all things around me.
> Everything seems grey and sombre, as when a fog blots out the sun and enshrouds the earth.
> Everything is an effort, everything is difficult.
> It wouldn't matter, except that I am alone.
> I am alone.

---

1 Genesis 1.2–4
2 John 8.12
3 John 13.30

You have taken me far Lord . . . you walked at my side . . .
and now, at night, in the middle of the desert, suddenly you
have disappeared . . .
Lord it is dark.
Lord are you here in my darkness?
Where are you Lord?
Do you love me still?
Or have I wearied you?
Lord answer,
Answer!
It is dark.[4]

Where is God – who is 'Light', 'Presence', 'Meaning', 'Love' –
when we cannot see our way, or when we feel alone, or when
we can see no pattern in what we are going through, or when we
sense no tender touch to reassure us that all is well? What has
God to say to us when night falls? Yet there is within Christian
tradition another expression of the significance of darkness that
suggests that despite the uncertainty and confusion, night holds
hidden gifts and opportunities.

One glad night

On the night of December 2nd 1577, Juan de Yepes y Alvarez, a
Carmelite friar, was seized and taken to a prison cell in Toledo,
where he was to spend the next nine months. His 'crime' was
his involvement in a movement aimed at restoring the lost vigour
of the Carmelite Order – a reform that threatened both religious
and political jurisdictions. The tiny cell had previously served as a
latrine; there was no window, only a narrow slit opening high up in
the wall. Whilst there, he was regularly humiliated and beaten by
members of his own religious community. Writing later, Juan – or
as history knows him, John of the Cross – likened the experience

---

4 Michel Quoist, 1965, excerpt from 'It is Dark' in *Prayers of Life*, Dublin:
Gill and Macmillan, published in North America as *Prayers* by Sheed and
Ward, an imprint of Rowman and Littlefield Publishers Inc.

to being 'swallowed up' by a whale, consumed within the darkness of its belly.[5] Abused by his brothers, seemingly abandoned by his God, torn by self doubt, John endured an all-encompassing darkness, physical and spiritual. It was night.

In the last months of his imprisonment his conditions eased; ink and paper were provided for him. Poetry of beauty and passionate intensity began to flow from within, expressing an unexpected gift: this 'tomb of dark death' had become for him a place of 'spiritual resurrection'.[6] Pushed to the edge by anguish and isolation, John tumbled beyond his own resources into deep, transforming *Presence*. I imagine John in the dark of his cell, alone. From somewhere outside he hears the faint sounds of voices and movement; closer by, the scuttling of a cockroach; and louder than all, the turmoil of his thoughts. His prayer seems to go nowhere, rebounding from the walls of his cell. He longs for inner stillness but is left with his own restlessness. Day and night merge as one. The sun forgets to rise. There is no one to hear his cry.

And then a day comes when Christ is there; quietly at first, but unmistakably *there*. Had he burst through the confining walls of fear and terror, or was he always with him? Just as when we are plunged from light into darkness, we see nothing at first, but slowly our eyes adjust, now sensing shapes that then begin to take real form so that we can name them for what they are. And this *Presence* for John was deeper, more intimate and more substantial than anything he had known before. The prison remained, the longing for kindly human companionship, the desire for physical freedom, the waves of sadness and frustration; and yet beyond all these the intuitive understanding that in everything he was held; nothing was finally lost; he was not alone. He wrote of the mysterious company of his Lord, recalled in the memory of the beautiful, but even more intensely discovered within the isolation of the night:

---

5 Letter to Catalina de Jesus, July 6th 1581. All quotations from John of the Cross are taken from: Kieran Kavanaugh and Otilio Rodriguez, 1991, *The Collected Works of John of the Cross*, translated and introduced by Kieran Kavanaugh and Otilio Rodriguez, Revised Edition, Washington D.C.: ICS Publications

6 The Dark Night, Book 2: 6.1

My Beloved, the mountains,
and lonely wooded valleys,
strange islands,
and resounding rivers,
the whistling of love-stirring breezes,

The tranquil night
at the time of the rising dawn,
silent music,
sounding solitude,
the supper that refreshes, and deepens love.[7]

He was later to write about the gift of this presence: 'Contemplation is nothing else than a secret and peaceful and loving inflow of God, which, if not hampered, fires the soul in the spirit of love.'[8] The experience of imprisonment – its stripping away of surface concerns and drawing down to his deepest longings – had given room for this 'inflow of God'. His ordeal was unanticipated, unwanted and unjust, and yet, through the gift of God, this time had expanded his inner being, creating wider horizons, drawing him into life-giving relationship. Of all his poems, *The Dark Night*, probably written shortly after his release from captivity, is perhaps the most personal, opening a window on this time that changed his life:

One dark night,
fired with love's urgent longings
– ah, the sheer grace! –
I went out unseen,
my house being now all stilled;

In darkness, and secure,
by the secret ladder, disguised,
– ah the sheer grace! –

---

7   Spiritual Canticle: stanzas 13–14
8   The Dark Night, Book 1: 10.6

in darkness and concealment,
my house being now all stilled.

On that glad night,
in secret, for no one saw me,
nor did I look at anything,
with no other light or guide
than the one that burned in my heart;

This guided me
more surely than the light of noon
to where he was awaiting me –
him I knew so well –
there in a place where no one appeared.

O guiding night!
O night more lovely than the dawn!
O night that has united
the Lover with his beloved
transforming the beloved in her Lover.[9]

The dark night is 'glad' and 'lovely'; darkness is 'secure'. Night
has awakened longing that burns in the heart and joins lover and
beloved, 'transforming the beloved in her Lover'. The meaning
eludes precise analysis and explanation, but the heartfelt feeling
expresses itself in breathless energy: night through 'sheer grace',
complete gift, has brought John a new joy and integration through
dimensions of relationship with God he could never have guessed
at before this experience. And this wholeness has come *through*
the night, not once the night was ended.

John eventually escaped his captors, loosening the screws of the lock
of his cell and stealing out at night, before lowering himself through
a window high above the river Tajo on a rope made from strips torn
from his bed covers. He risked death to find life and freedom. There
is, then, no suggestion that John glorified his imprisonment as a good

---

9 The poem 'The Dark Night', stanzas 1–5

in itself, or clung to this intense experience of suffering. God does not set out to make our existence miserable and nor should we. But suffering does happen as part of the stuff of life; there are times when control of our circumstances is taken from us. For John it was unjust imprisonment, and the silence that greeted his prayers for release. For you and me, 'night' may take some other shape. No one wants or looks for such nights, but they come, and John teaches us that painful as these experiences are, they may also bear unexpected gifts.

In darkness and secure

One of the most puzzling combinations of words within John's poem about his prison experience is: *in darkness and secure*. For most of us darkness is anything but secure. We cannot see where we are going, or exercise our usual control over our circumstances. Most of us naturally want to live in the daylight; that is, we prefer to be able to understand what is happening and have at least some power over the course of events. But paradoxically, might there be something restrictive about *always* being in the daylight – a confinement that keeps us in deep-down anxiety rather than true rest?

For as long as we are driven by our need to maintain control over what happens to us, we will live in fear of what might take place when we are not. I remember my trials and tribulations over learning to swim. I had no problem with waving my feet or arms about as long as some part of my anatomy was firmly attached to the side of the swimming pool. I was afraid of the water; I dare not launch out for fear that I would sink. And then one day I made a startling discovery: when I steeled myself to let go – and, as I expected, sank – I found that once *below* the surface I could swim. I pushed through the water smoothly, feeling its buoyancy. It was only when I was on the surface, and felt that staying afloat depended wholly on my frantic thrashing about, that panic set in. I came to understand that there was no reason to fear; if I sank I could swim. A new world was now open to me.

John uses another metaphor to explain how a life limited by fear can only be expanded by the choice to let go:

> To reach a new and unknown land . . . travellers cannot be guided by their own knowledge . . . they cannot reach new territory . . . if they do not take these new and unknown roads and abandon familiar ones.[10]

If I sink I will swim. If I abandon what is familiar and known I will find lands I do not know and cannot now see. It is the dark, not the light that holds the gift. True security comes not from keeping back the night, a task as futile as King Canute seeking to hold back the sea, but from learning to live with uncertainty and vulnerability: to be in darkness and secure.

John sits within an older tradition that understood that mystery is woven into the very experience of life and relationship. Who can comprehend entirely the wonder of birth, of inner transformation, or of death? Who in reality can keep control over the course of their life or build walls to successfully keep out the unexpected? And how can we begin to comprehend God, being utterly beyond us, even though intimately close to us? We do have real choices and it matters that we make them well, and we do have minds that equip us to wrestle with truth. But there are limits to our power, and truths beyond the grasp of our reasoning. Where these fail, a different response is needed: the risk of trust. I let go of the side and push out into the water.

It is this movement of trust I will go on to explore by drawing on John's reflections on the place of night within human and spiritual growth. But first I go back to that childhood wonder I was filled with before a truly dark and starlit night.

Turn off the lights

Nowadays – as long as we have enough shillings – we assert our power over darkness, lighting our houses and our streets. We can do more, and for longer; the benefits are clear. But if, like me, you are a star-gazer, this useful brightness awakes within us a certain lament: we have lost the wonder of a truly dark night. A new term

---

10 Dark Night, Book 2: 16.8

has entered our vocabulary: light pollution. In 2009, Galloway Forest Park was named the UK's first Dark Sky Park, an award set up by the International Dark Sky Association. Sark has recently become a 'dark sky island'; the Brecon Beacons National Park is setting out to gain similar status. Like the psalmist, we are beginning to recognize that it is good to feel small:

> When I look at your heavens, the work of your fingers,
> the moon and the stars that you have established;
> what are human beings that you are mindful of them,
> mortals that you care for them?[11]

To be wrapped in darkness, overcome by stars, is awesome, humbling, and grounding. But it is an experience few of us ever have. In collectively switching on the lights so that we can manage darkness, we have reduced night to something inconsequential, a pale shadow of the real and true. We no longer see stars.

For me it is a question of what we lose when we are too much in control. When we manage anything, whether it is a night sky or another person, to fit our own requirements, that 'other' is in some way diminished. We are no longer open to see the wonder, mystery, individuality and richness of objects beyond us. We make them what we need them to be and not what they are. Yet what they 'are' is so much more wonderful, if more dangerous, for not being formed by our desires and held in our power. In letting go control, we free ourselves to receive not what we decide we need, but what the other 'is'.

Perhaps then light pollution is a parable for what goes awry in our relationships. For another person is in a real sense 'a darkness', an unknown. If we see someone only in terms of their useful functionality in our world then what we see is a distortion. Most of us will have felt 'used'. When this happens it is as if the other person does not see us at all; they only perceive what is convenient to fit their needs. They lack the space and generosity to even want to know what we really think, feel and are. In the real world

---

11 Psalm 8.3–4

of course we do 'need'; we need encouragement, understanding, affirmation, and to feel wanted as much as we need bread, water and sleep. These are basic and healthy human longings that draw us to one another. Yet if we look to grab what we need at another's expense then what we seek eludes us, for the paradox is that we can only receive what we long for at this deep level of relationship without grasping it, as gift. Love is always a gift.

There is a place then for darkness: for letting the night sky *be* night sky and to pause before its wonder. There is a place within our relationships to receive the other as they are in their mystery rather than seek to fit who they are to suit us. If we are open to receive another as they are – whether this other is the created world we are part of, a person, or God – then layer upon layer of their richness will be unfolded to us, without ever coming to an end.

A journey by night

Later in his life John was asked to explain the meaning of his poems, and did so in a series of commentaries. Two connected works, *The Ascent of Mount Carmel* and *The Dark Night* rest on his poem, *The Dark Night*: the personal expression of the 'sheer grace' of his prison experience. Compared to the lightness of step of his verse, the language and tone of these works can seem heavy-footed and life-denying, so much so that on reading them as a nineteen-year-old I was not persuaded to return to them again for another thirty years! I got the wrong end of the stick, thinking that John's view of Christian life began and ended with self-denial and misery.[12] Life is demanding enough without going out and looking for difficulty. Instead John was inviting me to step out of my limited life to discover the richness of my humanity and the beauty of the created world around me. There was a catch: to find this freedom and fullness I would have to let go of my safe, familiar, self-controlled and self-oriented existence – and not once, but again and again at deeper

12 A helpful way in to the study of the writings of John of the Cross is provided by Iain Matthew's *The Impact of God: Soundings from St. John of the Cross*, 1995, London: Hodder and Stoughton

and deeper levels – until my life rested in a generosity and goodness I could not be sure existed until I took the risk of trusting it.

An encounter by night

> O night that has united
> the Lover with his beloved
> transforming the beloved in her Lover.

John does not suggest that painful or evil events that impact on us are good, or even directly sent by God, but that through them we can grow in the relational qualities that really matter: our capacity for large-hearted trust and love. These gifts open the way for what John calls 'union with God'. Some words of clarification are needed here: 'union with God' for John does not mean some measure of infinite perfection achieved by human effort. It is in these terms that the goal of Christian life is often described, with the suggestion that if we work at amending our behaviour and our thoughts we will one day attain a saintliness that makes us incapable of a single destructive impulse or action (I, for one, am still waiting!). The problem with this way of thinking is that it plays into our familiar pattern of wanting to climb the ladder of achievement by our own effort, independent of anyone else. 'Union' is a relational word: it is about interdependence, giving and receiving, the sharing of life; not something one-way or won.

A second area of potential misunderstanding is to see 'union with God' as solely belonging to the end of the spiritual journey. For John, the beginning, middle and end of the journey are about 'union with God'. What makes our life difficult is that we do not realize this union already exists and so do not allow our identity and being to flow from this source. God is not somewhere else, beyond our reach. God is within, though darkly. Everything to do with human growth, fruitfulness, integrity and creativity, John understands, is 'sheer grace', complete gift of God. Human effort remains, but this work is the active choice to enter into a relationship that from God's side is already given, and to continue to co-operate with God's giving until we are made complete. Union is about love: the choice of self-gift to another that belongs first to God but then also to us.

A third problem with the phrase 'union with God' might be the suggestion that it involves a private, self-indulgent happiness, independent of anything else happening in the world. What kind of worth can we give to a personal kingdom of contentment indifferent to the struggles of people outside it? There's nothing more off-putting than the 'pious' person who doesn't seem to care about people. But for John such a state of affairs would have very little to do with 'union with God'. The more we journey into relationship with God, the more we are drawn out in God into the world of people with their joys and pains. For God is other-centred love, ever alongside and ever at work to make what is broken whole. To realize fully our union with God is to become as God is. Again, the movement is away from self-absorption and into relationship that is self-generous.

What then, is the road to the realization in fullness of this 'union with God'? John draws from his experience to suggest that the experience of 'night' will play an important part:

We can offer three reasons for calling this journey towards union with God a night. The first has to do with the point of departure, because individuals must deprive themselves of their appetites for worldly possessions. This denial and privation is like a night for all one's senses. The second reason refers to the means or the road along which a person travels to this union. Now this road is faith, and for the intellect faith is also like a dark night.

The third reason pertains to the point of arrival, namely God. And God is also a dark night to the soul in this life. These three nights pass through a soul, or better, the soul passes through them in order to reach union with God . . .

These three nights comprise only one night, a night divided into three parts, like natural night. The first night, the night of the senses resembles early evening, that time of twilight when things begin to fade from sight. The second part, faith, is completely dark, like midnight. The third part, representing God, is like the very early dawn, just before the break of day.[13]

---

13 The Ascent of Mount Carmel, Book 1: 2.1, 5

The point of departure

The first (reason) has to do with the point of departure, because individuals must deprive themselves of their appetites for worldly possessions. This denial and privation is like a night for all one's senses.

Here John is thinking of a night we actively choose. Because we are so habitually rooted in the need to 'have' (control, the favour of others, our immediate wants . . .) the work of becoming free is difficult and unfamiliar. It is not that what we want is bad in itself, rather it is our 'appetites' for these things that are out of balance and need redirection.

Let me give you an example from my own experience. I worked out as a child that my way of fitting into my world was to meet others' expectations of me. I was deeply insecure about my worth, so sought favour by hiding away anything I thought might be unacceptable in their eyes: my true opinions, my feelings, my preferences. Whilst this might appear as admirable self-forgetfulness, in reality it was entirely about self-preservation. To an extent this determination to be a 'good boy' served me well, until I began to recognize it was like wearing a suit of clothes several sizes too small. I was living in a constricted and anxious world, driven by terror of disapproval and fear of the hidden 'real me' I had no opportunity to know. The 'point of departure' for me was the saying of a short and simple word: 'no'. Instead of fitting in, I opted to be true to what I really felt. A simple word had become a matter of life or death. To speak it was to enter a night-time world where I might meet myself, the person I most feared to know, and lose the approval that had hitherto kept me 'safe'; not to speak it, and to go on not speaking it, was to allow myself to shrivel up inside.

Jesus once shared a parable about a merchant searching in the marketplace for the finest of pearls; when he found it he gladly chose to sell everything he had to gain it. There is self-denial here, but self-denial that has reason and purpose. In the interests of our wholeness, freedom and long-term happiness we may choose to let go of what we once counted on. There are nights we enter into freely, for something within summons us to life and we know we must respond. We will remain stuck where we are unless we take 'new and unknown roads and abandon familiar ones'.[14]

The night of faith

The second reason refers to the means or the road along which a person travels to union. Now this road is faith, and for the intellect faith is also like a dark night.

So far John has been speaking about nights we choose, but what happens when night chooses us? In John's circumstances in prison, the power to influence anything was taken away, save this one thing: to seek to rest his life in a Love he could not feel and that seemed absent to him. The road John found in the dark night of his cell might be summed up like this: *'If I am to get anywhere, or become anything then it will be by your gift Lord, and so I will continue to place my life in your hands.'* It is night not to know whether the path one senses oneself drawn on leads anywhere; it is night to let go into God's hands and not be sure those 'hands' are there at all; it is night to set aside the activity of thought and enter into the stillness of prayer, when prayer seems empty and useless. Those situations that take us out of our depth, and beyond our normal pattern of control, make us most vulnerable. But what if instead of resisting this vulnerability we choose it, seeing it as an invitation to place our past, present and future within another's care? This way of faith might seem no more than resigned passivity. But I think of myself learning to swim, choosing between clinging to the rail on the side or launching out into the water. At the moment of letting go I chose to believe that if I swam the water would hold me up – a trust expressed in action though not in any measure felt. No effort could keep me from drowning should the water lack its natural buoyancy; but neither could I gain the freedom of swimming if I insisted on not letting go. Faith, John suggests, is the active choice, made not once but over and

---

14 Dark Night, Book 2: 16.8

again, to allow God to be the source of everything we are and will be – to let go and let God. It is a 'yes' to the vulnerable trust and openness that makes depth of relationship possible.

The darkness of God

The third reason pertains to the point of arrival, namely God. And God is also a dark night to the soul in this life.

God is intimately alongside us, yet utterly beyond our comprehension; light to us, yet also darkness, for any relationship has its element of mystery. We have seen already how we meet mystery in those experiences we cannot wholly understand. Beauty and suffering in different ways fill us with wonder and make us question our previous assumptions. We recognize that our understanding of the world has been too limited, and our map of reality too small. Mystery also meets us in those circumstances that we cannot control or make sense of but must live through, and in the questions that meet us in the course of life whose answers we begin to glimpse but cannot wholly capture. There are some things we know intuitively that elude adequate words of explanation. There is profound darkness in the understanding and expression of our experience; yet we know this darkness conceals true light.

We 'know' in different ways. There is a knowledge that comes from grasping abstract concepts – for example, that substances are made up of atoms. There is knowledge that comes second-hand: we read a biography of Nelson Mandela and so learn certain facts about his life. But we can know a great deal of factual information about someone and still not 'know' them. Fact-based or intellectually based knowing only carries us so far. A different quality of knowing comes through relationship, particularly when there is a depth of commitment between the two people. Paradoxically it may feel more difficult to describe what it is we know because this knowledge is at a deeper level and cannot be expressed wholly through mere words, no matter how high we pile them. We begin to glimpse, or sense, something of the heart of the other, without ever feeling we have understood all there is to know. Relational knowing is open-ended – a continuing journey of discovery. From time to time we realize that our previous assumptions were inadequate and have to be let go of, in order to come closer to a truth we will never wholly grasp. This is the way we 'know' God: for whilst we can learn many things about God – through the Bible, through sermons, even through a book like this one – we will never *capture* God in thoughts, concepts and ideas. Only in relationship with God will we begin the real journey of understanding. And then we will often feel out of our depth – because we are.

I think of Jesus' disciples desperately seeking to pin down who their master was and what was expected of them. No wonder they were sometimes a little confused: the one who is lord must be a servant; the one who humbles himself will be exalted; the first shall be last and the last first; those who seek to save their life will lose it, but those who lose it will save it; the one who gives away will receive. Jesus' life itself mirrored these paradoxes: a lord who washes people's feet; who befriends the sinner rather than the righteous; who dies a criminal's death on a dark Friday afternoon and so becomes the source of life for all. Those who enter into relationship with God experience dark night every bit as much as bright day. Yet the darkness is not an absence of light; it is a superabundance of light so bright it dazzles us so that we cannot see.

Three nights in one night

These three nights pass through a soul, or better the soul passes through them in order to reach union with God. These three nights comprise only one night, a night divided into three parts, like natural night. The first night, the night of the senses resembles early evening, that time of twilight when things begin to fade from sight. The second part, faith, is completely dark, like midnight. The third part, representing God, is like the very early dawn, just before the break of day.

It might seem that John is suggesting a linear progress through different stages of darkness. Yet as John suggests, these three experiences are intertwined, inseparable dimensions of one night.

We never stop recognizing that in order to live we have to leave behind what is familiar, secure, yet deadening, and risk the difficult and unknown path. We express trust in action by letting go and letting God in situations where we cannot see the way ahead and lack the control to bring about change by ourselves. And the whole is a journey into the darkness of God whereby we are led into the hitherto unknown light of our being.

Night-works

Night is the favoured time for improvements and repairs taking place on the Underground or on the motorways. They often seem to take longer than anticipated. As night falls the body grows weary of its activity, demanding our relinquishment into passivity, pressing us towards necessary rest. Our dreams will redraw the mind's day. Night falls and Jesus' life is no longer in his hands. In the quiet of a garden he prays for what will be accomplished before morning comes.

When we look back we may well see that night has been a catalyst for significant life changes. It is far harder to draw positive sense and meaning from events at the time. Night will probably be something we endure more than rejoice in. Yet night holds its unexpected gifts for those willing to open their hands to receive them. Sometimes – in prayer and in life – we walk in the daylight. When we pray we sense God's nearness; though life has its challenges we sense it is going somewhere and we have a say in its direction. At other times we find ourselves plunged into night. We seek to pray but prayer seems empty of satisfaction, empty of God. Darkness has come down suddenly; our assumptions about the future collapse. We have no coin for the meter. Yet God holds us, and though hidden in its depths, the night holds God.

For reflection:

1] Starry, starry night

Night – truly dark night away from the glare of street lamps – enables us to see the beautiful light of stars usually hidden from us in daytime.

At night, some lights shine more brightly. Perhaps when you look back at your own times of struggle and sorrow you can also glimpse hidden lights emerging from that night:

- A sense of the presence of God alongside or within you, not taking away sorrow but holding you within it.
- A truer understanding of who you are and what really matters in life.
- A deeper awareness of the beauty and wonder of life.
- Gratitude for love given.
- A new sense of direction.

Gaze afresh at those stars once shown to you at night and give God thanks.

2] Dark sky space

Spend some time in a physical 'dark sky space'. You might arrange to go with others deep into the country, or find somewhere near you away from street lamps: a park or open space, or even the back of your garden. Allow the night to soak into you. If there are stars, spend some time gazing at them, noticing their different colours and brightness.

3] Prayer of presence

Prayer is not always about words. It can also be a quiet 'being with' God in which we put aside thoughts and words and simply seek to be present, aware and attentive. We step into the darkness of the unknown that is God.

- **Be comfortable:** Sit comfortably with your feet on the ground and your hands at rest in your lap or by your side. Close your eyes.
- **Listen:** Listen to the sounds of this space: the hum of distant traffic, the creak of floorboards, your own breathing. Rather than thinking too much, give all your attention to what you

can hear, and when you feel drawn away from this by your worries and concerns, go back to this relaxed listening and awareness. After time and with practice, you will find yourself stilling down into an inner quiet.

· **Seek God:** God is in this place; God is in this moment. God is here, God is now. You are here to be open to this presence. Perhaps you will find yourself expressing this in a simple prayer, or in a gesture such as opening your hands.

· **Use a prayer word:** You may find it helps to hold a prayer word or short phrase before you in this time to express your seeking (for example: 'Lord, I seek you', or, 'Bless the Lord O my soul'). Use your prayer word as helpful to keep you in stillness: now quietly repeating it, now falling into silence.

· **Get into the practice:** Commit yourself to spending ten minutes a day in this way. At a later stage you may want to increase this.

· **Don't worry about results:** The aim of this prayer is not to have great thoughts or even feel God's closeness. You may feel nothing or even feel bored. Don't try too hard – everything is gift.

3

Jacob Wrestling

The same night he got up and took his two wives, his two maids and his eleven children, and crossed the ford of the Jabbok. He took them and sent them across the stream, and likewise everything that he had. Jacob was left alone, and a man wrestled with him until daybreak. When the man saw that he did not prevail against Jacob, he struck him on the hip socket, and Jacob's hip was put out of joint as he wrestled with him. Then he said, 'Let me go, for the day is breaking.' But Jacob said, 'I will not let you go unless you bless me.' So he said to him, 'What is your name?' And he said, 'Jacob'. Then the man said, 'You shall no longer be called Jacob, but Israel, for you have striven with God and with humans and have prevailed.' Then Jacob asked him, 'Please tell me your name.' But he said, 'why is it that you ask my name?' And there he blessed him. So Jacob called the place Peniel, saying, 'for I have seen God face to face, and yet my life is preserved.' The sun rose upon him as he passed Penuel, limping because of his hip. (Genesis 32: 22–31)

Jacob wrestled with God, refusing to let go until he received a blessing. The story is in part about names. We learn that Jacob is *Israel* – literally 'one who strives with God'. We discover that *Penuel*, the place of meeting is so-called because here Jacob met God face to face.[1] Yet this is far more than a story about the origin of words. It tells us of identity gained through struggle. The conflict takes place at a crossing point between one side of the river and the other, and

---

1 The literal meaning of the Hebrew *Penuel* is 'face of God'.

between the past and the future. Jacob receives a new name and a new beginning. Neither party in the struggle will let go: Jacob of God or God of Jacob. Jacob, now *Israel*, goes away as the sun rises, limping from the encounter but also transformed.

Conflict is part of our human existence: we know its familiar roots in a mismatch of expectations, a struggle for control or a divergence of attitudes. Conflicts are most difficult and painful when our 'opponent' is someone important to us: a friend, a partner or a family member. The issue is the catalyst for the struggle, but what comes into question is the very nature of the relationship: 'Can I really trust this person? Is she who I thought she was or have I got her completely wrong? Is this "make" or "break"?' These may well be the very questions that come into play when our conflict is not with another person but with God. However, whilst conflict is disturbing, it often opens the way for deeper mutual understanding and a more fruitful relationship. Real intimacy is rarely achieved without at some stage having to work through differences, or one or both parties having to adjust their behaviour and attitudes to make room for the other. Honesty often hurts, but it is essential. Without it relationships can drift along or drift apart at a level of superficial niceness. With honesty we own and express real emotions. The potential exists to grow into a new level of understanding if both sides are willing to stay with the struggle and to have faith in the essential goodness of the other.

Jacob wrestled and did not let go, and neither did the stranger who held him in his grasp. The relationship with God, even more than one with another human being, is ripe ground for misunderstanding. As intimately as God comes alongside us, God continually transcends our assumptions and escapes our efforts to manipulate and control. 'As the heavens are higher than the earth, so are my ways higher than your ways, and my thoughts than your thoughts', God declares through the prophet Isaiah.[2] Our hold on who God is proves too small, and we have either to ditch the effort to grow in our understanding or let ourselves be led

---

2 Isaiah 55.8

along paths we do not know to a new level of insight, that in time will again prove inadequate. Yet God is doing no more than be honest with us, for he values us and is wholly committed to relationship with us. Can we bring the same level of honesty and commitment in return?

Say it as it is

There are no 'good' and no 'bad' emotions. What we feel simply 'is'. This might be standard stuff for you but for me it was a revolutionary insight. In the family I grew up in the mention of any emotion was enough to send all diving behind the sofa! When my mother really detested something she would say, 'it's quite nice'. Perhaps it is unsurprising that I grew up understanding that strong emotions like anger were always wrong and inappropriate; and so I set out to deny their existence in me. I firmly believed I was not an angry person until someone so persistently got under my skin that I finally exploded with rage – much to his surprise and mine.

There was a period of time when I found it quite impossible to pray. I sat in quiet but felt the space claustrophobic; I couldn't settle. I read the words of the Bible but their meaning trailed off into nothingness. Until the day when I understood that I was too angry to pray – at least too angry to pray in any way that demanded passivity. I was up to here with God, asking innumerable things of me but not caring one jot about me and my needs. I was continually tripping over pains I had unsuccessfully attempted to bury, taking out my fury on inanimate objects when they refused to work. Finally I began to tell God what I thought. It wasn't what I had thought of as prayer up to then (since when has swearing counted as prayer?). But as time went on there began to be quiet spaces amidst the raging. I saw it was I, more than God, who had set myself up to be so put upon and, surprisingly, it was God who was inviting me to do something about it.

I remember Rabbi Lionel Blue telling the story of a woman coming to his synagogue for the first time. It was a new experience for her and she wanted to get things right. She dressed smartly, found what felt like a safe place amongst the congregation, tried to work out when to rise and fall and when to speak or stay silent as the service progressed. And then she dropped her handbag, spilling its contents noisily on to the floor. She swore. And that was the moment, according to Lionel Blue, when she began to pray. Prayer has to be real or it is nothing at all. God doesn't require that we be on best behaviour or give an edited version of ourselves free of the parts that we judge unsavoury or undesirable. Honesty is all.

I find it reassuringly counter-cultural that the Bible contains the Psalms. If God, or the Church, had wanted to do a PR job on the Bible to ensure that only those parts that glorified God or praised his goodness made it into the final text they would have surely cut the Psalms out. Instead, there they are, openly questioning God: doubt, anger, loneliness, fear, confusion, a desperate sense of God's rejection – it is all there, laid bare, preserved in holy writ. Yet praise, trust, joy, thanksgiving are also mixed in, and often in the same psalm:

> How long, O lord? Will you forget me for ever?
> How long will you hide your face from me?
> How long must I bear pain in my soul
> and have sorrow in my heart all day long?
> . . . But I trusted in your steadfast love;
> my heart shall rejoice in your salvation.
> I will sing to the Lord,
> because he has dealt bountifully with me.[3]

The very fact that the feelings are named, the despair voiced, is testament to the strength of the relationship. No one walks away in a final way from God, and despite feelings, those who share their pain also know somewhere that God has not walked out on them. They do not understand and they feel let down, but they are still in there questioning and questing. Jacob wrestled with God, refusing to let go until he received a blessing.

---

3 Psalm 13.1–2, 5–6

Send my roots rain

Gerard Manley Hopkins is principally known for his poems celebrating the wonder of a God-created world – As kingfishers catch
fire, Pied Beauty, The Windhover among them. The 'Terrible' or
'Dark' sonnets written whilst Hopkins was Professor of Greek
Literature at University College, Dublin have a very different
flavour. His mind-numbing work in a rundown university in
what was then a dirty, poverty-stricken city physically and men-
tally exhausted him. Writing of this period to his friend Bridges,
Hopkins remarked, 'my spirits were so crushed that madness
seemed to be making approaches.'[4] Hopkins was far from friends
and family, removed from the countryside that fed his spirit and
haunted by the seeming lack of fulfilment of his potential as poet,
priest and human being. Posting had followed posting without
him ever sensing he had found his place or that what he offered
was welcomed and understood by those he lived with and ministered to. Now, in what he called 'this winter world', he mourned
the loss of the 'roll, the rise, the carol, the creation' of his earlier
poetic work.[5] He wrote of how 'the melancholy I have all my life
been subject to has become of late years . . . more distributed,
constant and crippling.'[6]

Hopkins struggled to make sense of what was happening in his
life. Was his affliction divinely initiated to free him from undue
attachments? Or was it designed to heal him of his faults, so that
his 'chaff might fly' and his 'grain lie, sheer and clear?'[7] 'Why
do sinners' ways prosper', he complained, and 'why must disap-

---

4 Claude Colleer Abbott (ed.), 1935, *The Letters of Gerard Manley
Hopkins to Robert Bridges*, London: Oxford University Press, p. 222.

5 The definitive edition of Hopkins' poetry is probably *The Poems of
Gerard Manley Hopkins*, Fourth Edition, revised and enlarged, 1967,
Edited by W.H. Gardner and N.H. MacKenzie, Oxford: Oxford University
Press. Numberings of poems follow this edition. This poem is *To R.B*,
poem 76.

6 Claude Colleer Abbott (ed.), 1956, *Further Letters of Gerard Manley
Hopkins*, London: Oxford University Press, p. 256.

7 Poem 64

pointment all I endeavour end?' And yet this 'why' is addressed to 'thou my friend'.[8] However haltingly, Hopkins continued in his calling as a poet and a priest, always facing the God he knew to be the heart of all existence. God seemed absent; Hopkins' cries were 'like dead letters sent to dearest him that lives alas! away.'[9] Yet he held together his feelings of abandonment and confusion with enduring faith in the underlying goodness of God; he was still 'dearest him'. If God was silent, both passive and active in ways he could not fathom, Hopkins knew he had no other way, no other truth, no other source of life than God: 'Mine, O thou Lord of life', he prayed, 'send my roots rain'.[10]

Hopkins felt bewildered and pained in his unknowing, yet remained faithful in his commitment to God. In these sonnets Hopkins is like Jacob, wrestling through the night with a stranger, refusing to let go until he grants him his blessing. He looks back to an earlier time of struggle, wondering who it was right to support. Should he be on his own side or on that of Christ? Was there something won then and something to be won now in not having things his way?

> Cheer whom though? The hero whose heaven-handling flung me, foot trod
> Me? or me that fought him? O which one? Is it each one? That night, that year
> Of now done darkness I wretch lay wrestling with (my God!) my God.[11]

The wrestling was not only with God but also with his own temptation to despair; and was this in reality Christ within striving to overthrow Hopkins' own impulse for self-destruction?

> Not, I'll not, carrion comfort, Despair, not feast on thee;

---

8 Poem 74
9 Poem 67
10 Poem 74
11 Poem 64 *Carrion Comfort*

Not untwist – slack they may be – these last strands of man
In me or most weary cry I can no more. I can:
Can something, hope, wish day come, not choose not to be.[12]

If we cannot summon up the hope that despite current circumstances all will be well, at least we can choose to turn ourselves
in hope's direction and away from the quicksand of despair. We
see this movement within Psalm 22 where the piercing cry 'My
God, my God, why have you forsaken me?' is held together with
the remembrance of God's goodness, for: 'he did not hide his face
from me but heard when I cried to him.'[13]

There comes a moment when Hopkins grasps that it is in letting go to God, in the absence of understanding, that the struggle
begins to be won. God's comfort, he realizes, cannot be grasped,
for it arrives as a gift, at the unexpected moment:

. . . Let joy size
At God knows when to God knows what, whose smile's not
wrung, see you'.[14]

I do not let go of God; I hold on to my question and I give him my
pain. Yet at the same time I release my grip on having my question
answered at this moment, or my hurt healed in this particular
way. 'God knows when to God knows what' is not a bitter 'well,
I'll believe it when I see it!' It is an acknowledgement that life is
not entirely in our hands, and that trust in the ultimate generosity
of life and of God must have a place. The phrase is echoed in one
of Hopkins' most exuberant affirmations of the enduring beauty
and surprise of all that God brings into being:

All things counter, original, spare, strange;
Whatever is fickle, freckled (who knows how?)
With swift, slow; sweet, sour; adazzle, dim;

---

12 Poem 64 *Carrion Comfort*
13 Psalm 22.1, 24
14 Poem 69

He fathers-forth whose beauty is past change:
Praise him.[15]

The mood of the two poems is very different, but the truth expressed is the same: God is continually creative, yet elusively beyond our control: therefore make room for his unexpected and un-won giving.

Letting go to God also involves relinquishing self-loathing. There is a temptation, when we are most under stress, to turn inward and unpick ourselves, thread by thread, fault by fault, shortcoming by shortcoming, until there is nothing left to love or value. Instead, a little gentleness creates 'root room' for God's comfort. He tells himself:

My own heart let me have more pity on; let
Me live to my sad self hereafter kind,
Charitable; not live this tormented mind
With this tormenting mind tormenting yet.[16]

Paradox is writ large in this poetry: absence wrestles with intimacy, questioning with trust, resistance with submission. Hopkins does not let go of God, and knows that God has never, and will never, let go of him. In the midst of the unwinding and disintegration of life and meaning the resurrection explodes:

In a flash, at a trumpet crash
I am all at once what Christ is, since he was what I am, and
This Jack, joke, poor potsherd, patch, matchwood, immortal
diamond
Is immortal diamond.[17]

---

15 Poem 37, *Pied Beauty*
16 Poem 69
17 Poem 72, *That Nature is a Heraclitean Fire and of the Comfort of the Resurrection*

Hopkins once described mystery as 'incomprehensible certainty'.[18] We wrestle with what cannot be grasped with our mind or controlled by our will. There are no simplistic answers, no easy solutions. And yet there is God present, and in some way beyond our understanding, active within this suffering. There is the certainty of Love that refuses to let us go. If we hold on with Jacob we will receive blessing.

Throw away thy wrath

George Herbert was another priest-poet. Like Hopkins his fixed reference point for exploring his experience and feelings was his relationship with God. His prayer flowed into his poetry and his poetry often has the quality of prayer. Herbert's work has an intimate and conversational quality. We know he is speaking and yet as he does so, he provides words for our experience. In common with Hopkins he wrote to make sense of his own life, but also to give us some footholds for understanding ours. He too is a Jacob figure, unable to loose himself from the grasp God has on his life and determined to hold God to account for his actions – or lack of them. His life is 'bitter-sweet':

> Ah my dear angrie Lord,
> Since thou dost love, yet strike;
> Cast down, yet help afford;
> Sure, I will do the like.
> I will complain, yet praise;
> I will bewail, approve;
> And all my sour-sweet days
> I will lament and love.[19]

Opposites belong together in no way that makes sense but yet is real. God is love and yet we hurt. We question his care because

---

18 Abbott, 1935, p. 187–8
19 *Bitter-Sweet*

we know he does care. Even as we complain some other part of us
dares to believe we are held in love. Sometimes, however, the pain
is great and there is no other way except to express it:

> Broken in pieces all asunder
> Lord hunt me not,
> A thing forgot,
> Once a poor creature, now a wonder.
> A wonder tortured in the space
> Betwixt this world and that of grace.[20]

In his poem *The Collar*, Herbert expresses his rage not only at
God but at his own inability to step outside the constraints of the
relationship. He strikes the table and cries 'no more'. Hasn't he
the freedom to go where he wills? What has God ever brought
him? Why not simply seek enjoyment wherever he can find it and
forget thoughts about what is right or wrong, or what obliga-
tions he owes to other people? And then, amidst the violence of
his assault, he senses God's gentle call to him and finds himself
responding:

> But as I rav'd and grew more fierce and wilde
> At every word,
> Me thoughts I heard one calling, *Child*;
> And I reply'd, *My Lord*.

There is storm and somewhere – usually hidden so deep we are
unaware of it – there is calm. At one point in the Gospel story the
disciples are seized with fear as a gale rages on the Sea of Galilee,
threatening to overwhelm their boat; meanwhile Jesus sleeps. 'Why
don't you do something?' they cry; 'we are perishing!'[21] At the
heart of the account is not the dead calm that falls upon the waters
at Jesus' command but the figure of Jesus asleep amidst the turmoil.

---

20 Excerpt from *Affliction* (iv)
21 Mark 4.35–9

Perhaps we are both sides of this story, calling out our confusion and anxiety as the storm rages but also at rest in the stern of the boat. With Herbert we rave and grow fierce and wild, but then also sense one calling our name and find it within ourselves to respond 'My Lord'.

We cannot shortcut the process of coming to a place of trust by denying the presence of doubt and fear. Even when some part of us is able to reason that God is not directly responsible for what we are going through, still there is some human need to say that it is so. We cannot help but expect that God should answer our prayer and deliver us from our need in ways that we can clearly see and in terms that are immediately understandable. Something as trivial as standing late at night in a desolate place waiting for the right number bus to come by and take me home can drive me into complaint against God: 'Why don't you bring a number 96; every other bus in the world has passed by?' No wonder I cannot handle the deeper crises of life! Herbert urges God to deal with him more gently, remembering his all-too-human vulnerability:

Throw away thy rod
Throw away thy wrath:
O my God,
Take the gentle path . . .

Though I fail, I weep;
Though I halt in pace,
Yet I creep
To the throne of grace

Then let wrath remove
Love will do the deed;
For with love
Stony hearts will bleed . . .

Throw away thy rod
Though man frailties hath,

Thou are God:
Throw away thy wrath.[22]

Say it how it feels – the relationship is well founded enough to take it. God receives our cries, even when they are of pain, doubt and challenge rather than joy and praise. Life and God are too deep, wide and long to always be made sense of by simple reasoning. We have to stay with what is and not run away; but it is hard to do so without having somewhere to place our hurt and confusion. Yet there is joy, there is presence; often found in the most unlikely places and amidst unpromising times:

And now in age I bud again,
After so many deaths I live and write;
I once more smell the dew and rain,
And relish versing: O my only light
It cannot be
That I am he
On whom thy tempests fell at night.[23]

Jacob and the joust

We go back another 400 years and find another poet who turned to the image of Jacob wrestling to express the difficulty of being in relationship with God in circumstances that challenge our understanding. Hadewijch used the imagery of the then popular literature of 'courtly love', combined with biblical themes, to explore the experience of God, and in particular how suffering plays a part in spiritual growth. Central to the ballads of courtly love was the theme of the lowly knight pursuing a desirable, noble Lady. The Lady is elusive, encouraging the knight's advances, but then withdrawing her favours. The knight has to prove his worth by his valour in deeds and the persistence of his search in the face of obstacles and lack of encouragement. Within Hadewijch's poetry,

---

22 Excerpt from *Discipline*
23 Excerpt from *The Flower*

God is therefore a 'she' – Lady Love – and her seeming lack of encouragement expresses the experience of encounter with God who is always present to us yet beyond our grasp, summoning us to a deeper love. The God-who-is Love yearns for us and draws us into relationship, awakening our desire. We may begin our search looking for the happiness this relationship gives us, but God draws us deeper, challenging us to love as God loves: freely, and purely for the other rather than for any return. The seeming absence of reward then presses us to go further, deeper; to let go of a lesser love and to open ourselves to the Love that is God. In another layer of courtly love imagery, this theme is played out in Hadewijch's writing through the language of the joust. God challenges us to join battle; to match Love with love. And just as Jacob overcame God through his persistence and received a new name and blessing, so we are challenged to seek not what God gives, but God alone, and so allow the Love that is God to flow through us.

But there is a twist in Hadewijch's understanding of the nature of the contest. In a joust or a wrestling match the combatants use their physical strength and guile to overcome their opponent; one looks to dominate and overthrow the other. But in this instance it is love that is the power used, and love by its nature does not seek to make the other subservient. Instead love desires to give itself for the other's sake. If this is a contest of love, other strengths come into play: generosity, the willingness to be vulnerable, the risk of trust, the capacity to move away from self-absorption to appreciate the other for herself rather than as an object to meet personal need. There is no more powerful player in this struggle than God herself, whom Hadewijch names as 'Love'.

'Love' is made known and present in the humble Christ: – as vulnerable as a baby in a mother's arms; as generous as the young man sitting down and eating with tax collectors and sinners, refusing to treat people according to label but calling them by name. Love is as unconditional and courageous as Jesus in the garden of Gethsemane, alone and afraid, yet refusing to turn back from giving all, even life itself, so that the loved one – you and I – might live. Hadewijch sees Christ's life as the pouring out in time of the eternal name of Love. When we are loved so much, and

without condition, how are we to respond? Have we the desire
and the courage to receive this love for what it is and to seek to
return it? This, Hadewijch sees, is the summons to the joust, and
in one of her poems she gives the loved one's reply:

> I greet you Love, with undivided love,
> And I am brave and daring,
> I will yet conquer your power,
> Or I will lose myself in the attempt![24]

But the one who responds to this challenge will not find it easy.
As the first letter to John says, love is 'not mere words and talk';
love is proved in deeds.[25] Whilst 'falling in love' is easy, growing
into true love for another is often a painful struggle. In relation to God: can I choose to be with God in prayer when the
activity ceases to reward me – when there is no feeling of peace
or enlightenment? Will I purposefully go out of myself to seek
the God who is ever in search of me? In relation to God met
in my fellow human beings: am I able to be free enough from
my own need to see and respond to yours? Can I allow you to
be the person you are rather than the one who fits into my life
conveniently? Am I generous enough to share what I have with
you even when there's nothing in it for me? There is another
wrestling going on here: a contest with the needy, self-centred
'me'. It is easy to take the first few steps along this road, but am
I committed to travel it for as long and as far as it asks of me?
Such love is ultimately God's gift, but asks our continual openness to seek and practise it:

---

24 Hadewijch texts are taken from Mother Columba Hart O.S.B.,
1980, *Hadewijch: the Complete Works*, translation and introduction by
Mother Columba Hart, preface by Paul Monmaers, New York: Paulist
Press. Abbreviations used in citing texts are PS. (Poems in Stanza), PC.
(Poems in Couplets), L. (Letters). This text is PS. 21.

25 John 3.18

One is held by sweet constraint to be in perpetual exertion, and with never-conquered power, to be a match for this Being; and – strong and unconquered and joyful – by ardent striving to grow up as loved one in the Beloved . . . to work with his hands, to walk with his feet, to hear with his ears . . . to live as the loved one in the Beloved, with the same way of acting, with one spirit, and with one heart.[26]

What will be the result of the struggle? Hadewijch turns things on their head again. The one who 'wishes to wrestle with God must set himself to conquer in order to be conquered.'[27] One must focus one's whole being on going all out for God and yet completely let go and surrender, for it is the one who allows 'Love to conquer him' who then will 'conquer Love completely'[28] and the one who is 'overpowered' who will 'overcome the . . . power never yet overthrown.'[29] Love is not a working *against* another but an offering of oneself *for* the other. It is the giving through which we receive. God vulnerably and generously shares everything with us; can we do the same?

As I sit at my computer today, typing, how do I meet Hadewijch's words? I don't think I would last long in an actual joust; I would fall off my horse without any assistance from my opponent – that is if I could get on it in the first place! But the thought behind the image will not go away so easily. In Hadewijch's time, to be summoned to a joust was to be treated as an equal; it was considered bad chivalry to challenge someone of lower rank. In loving me God invites me to grow into my own capacity for love. The summons is given; will I let fear, laziness or mediocrity stand in my way? If the way proves too hard will I step off it and find myself a comfortable seat? What would thereby be lost – not just for myself but for those whose lives are intertwined with mine? I am not thereby considering my life any

---

26 L. 30
27 L. 12
28 L. 19
29 PS. 19

more vital than anyone else's; the invitation reaches out to all. But no one else can answer the challenge for me; no one else can live my life – or yours.

Jacob refused to let go until the stranger gave him his blessing. It belongs to us to stay true to the contest; it belongs to God to call us by a new name and to grant us abundance of life. Prayer, however dry and unrewarding it may become, is transformational. The being of God is the source of our being. We grow into a humanity that is Christ-shaped yet distinctly 'our-shaped'. We discover and live out our name. 'I came', Jesus declared, 'that they may have life and have it abundantly';[30] but this life is given only through our willingness to seek it and our openness to the creative work of the Spirit within. We have to stay true to the engagement and not turn away.

Prayer is not just turning to God when we recognize our need for help or pouring out our thoughts and feelings in moments of joy or sorrow, but choosing to be present to God as a way of life. The author of Psalm 27 speaks of the search for God as the centre of his being: 'Come, my heart says, "seek his face". Your face O lord do I seek.'[31] Prayer is about life-orientation – the direction we choose to face – expressed through regular and chosen *times* of prayer. For Hadewijch prayer in her youth was energising and enjoyable; she tangibly felt God alongside her and saw the fruit of what she sought in prayer. As an older person prayer was often more difficult; a sense of God's presence less immediately accessible. Yet she had chosen God as her centre and the way to give this expression was to consciously open herself to God's presence in prayer. Like Jacob, she would not let go when ease and comfort slipped away. Those who engage in the combat with Love must stay in close relationship, allowing Love to look at them as they look at Love.

What does this abundant life look like? It is not a static and private bliss. It is being the best of who you are, freely and generously – and as yet you only know a little of what you are capable

---

30 John 10.10
31 Psalm 27.8–9

of. It is to create rather than to destroy, to heal rather than to hurt, to come alongside rather than to distance, and to build relationship rather than divide; or as Hadewijch declares, it is to not live less than what Love is:

> The greatest radiance anyone can have on earth is truth in works of justice in imitation of the Son. For he who gazes on what he desires, becomes ardently enkindled, so that his heart within him begins to beat slowly because of the sweet burden of Love. And through perseverance in this holy life of contemplation, wherein he continually gazes on God, he is drawn within God.[32]

To gaze on God is to centre your attentiveness on the Love that is God, expressed in Christ; it is to be drawn to, and feel within, the slow deep heartbeat of Love at the heart of everything. You can gaze on God through reading the Gospels, or gaze on God by being present to the wonder of the created world and the creator it expresses. You can gaze on God by your openness to people in their need, and in thankfulness for their generosity to you. We see God in all things, and then little by little we see all things in God. We hear God's heartbeat; and then God's heart beats within ours, producing 'truth in works of justice in imitation of the Son'.

Jacob speaks

It has not always been an easy relationship with God. On my part there have sometimes been harsh words. I have not always understood God's silence when I needed words, or unwillingness to intervene when I needed an answer. Yet I am still in there. Strangely too, I am more than ever convinced of God's commitment to me. The words of the Creed have leapt from the page into the heart. I sense God creativity everywhere about me. I find God alongside me, embracing my vulnerability. I trust, however haltingly, in God's continual labour to make me whole. Perhaps

---

32 L. 18

it is because I begin to see these same movements within me and I know this is the making of me: it is what makes life worthwhile, purposeful and beautiful. It is my only way to 'be'.

I am not done with wrestling because God is not done with me. What do I expect: that God will be entirely amenable to me and predictable? Someone or something that I can sum up and know all there is know about and so control to my own ends? Or someone whose depths I can only begin to guess at? Someone whose presence in my life challenges me to move out of a limited view of myself and take the adventure into the person I might become? If I take on the adventure then I also take on the danger and the pain it will sometimes bring. God has chosen this path with me and often with limited reward. I can do no less than choose the same. Though limping, I choose the blessing. Jacob will not let go.

For reflection:

1] Like Jacob we sometimes engage in struggle with God, expressing our questions, doubts and feelings. God will not be manipulated into doing what we wish, but then neither will God manipulate us. The psalms express a mixture of doubt and belief, praise and questioning, pain and joy. Many of the psalms seem to flow from a particular context faced by the individual or his people. Write your own psalm from the place where you are today. You too may have conflicting thoughts and emotions, see-sawing between hope and anxiety, faith and doubt; let this flow unchecked into your psalm.

2] Read the account of Jacob wrestling in Genesis 32: 22–31; it might help to read the whole chapter to put this encounter in context. Let the story take you back into your own experience of wrestling with God, past or present. What has been the fruit of this encounter? What have you discovered about yourself, or about God? What – if any – blessing have you received? Or have you been left limping?

3] What poems or prose have provided words for your own conversation with God in the past? Revisit any of these that particularly come to mind. How do they speak to you now?

4

The Hazel in Winter

It is December. Snow lies upon the ground. Daytime is bright with the low sun and night-time still and frosty. The trees are largely bare – or at first glance so; at second glance I see the catkin curls waiting to bloom on hazel bushes and fat buds on horse chestnuts. Any sense of settled seasons has been undermined for me: winter always holds, if hidden well, a hint of spring, just as I recognize the first scents of autumn on opening the door on mornings of what will be hot August days. True, there are times when day follows day of settled weather and it seems that the familiar turning of the world has stopped: the oppressive heat of mature summer or the wintering wind from the north east that interrupts spring in February and March. Eventually, however, these hesitations let go to the rhythm of the seasons that keeps time for our lives. The day is shorter or longer; the rising sun stretches high enough to warm a garden long held in shadow; the swallow takes flight and does not return.

If there is some sense of order in the seasons of the earth we may experience less within the seasons of the heart. Put simply, we do not know what is coming next. What we do know is that change will happen, whether chosen or unbidden – sometimes in a moment, and sometimes so gradually that we fail to notice until we find ourselves in quite a different place. I think of my leaving home to go to university, a move I anticipated as positive and life enhancing but that became the season when all my held-in anxiety about whether or not I had a rightful place in the universe became a quicksand of darkness and fear. I wasn't having the good time that had been promised. I couldn't do the work and I wasn't making lasting friendships. I had panic attacks in a crowd and felt isolated and unhappy when alone. And then a slow spring-time. I reached out to God in desperation and gradually began to recognize him already alongside me. Love was real; I was valued as I was; there was no need to be afraid. I flourished, finding my meaning in helping others who doubted their worth to begin to believe in themselves. God would work *everything* out – which was all very well until God didn't! I was back in a struggle again.

As unpredictable as they are, most of us do have these seasons. So where is God amidst this ebb and flow of our fortunes and feelings? Typically God is described as unchangeably removed from creation, subject as it is to continual change and decay:

> We blossom and flourish as leaves on the tree,
> And wither and perish—but naught changeth thee.[1]

'Naught changeth thee' might be all very well for God but it is a little remote from our experience. Nothing much stays the same in our outward or inward world. If I am happy today and sense that all is going well I am equally likely to be thrown into confusion by events tomorrow and not see any way my difficulties can be resolved. We are seasonal creatures, and the weather outside and inside is generally changeable! Yet is this understanding of an unchanging God altogether true or helpful? The static is usually insensitive or dead. Is this really the way of the living God? And is our changeability a sign of our inadequacy and immaturity, or the natural path of our life and growth, echoing what we see in creation?

Hadewijch and the seasons

> In the beginning Love always contents us
> When Love first spoke to me of love,
> O how with all that I was I greeted all that she is!

---

1 From the hymn: *Immortal, invisible, God only wise*, words: Walter Smith, 1876.

But then she made me resemble the hazelnut trees
That bloom early in the dark season,
And whose fruit one must wait a long time.[2]

Hadewijch, a spiritual guide and poet living in the Rhineland in the thirteenth century, drew parallels between the passing of the seasons and her own experience of life and of God. She was a Beguine – a member of a lay, female Christian community devoted to contemplative prayer and the service of the poor. Little detail is known about her life, and that we do know is glimpsed obliquely through her letters and poems. It seems that as a young woman she sensed God's presence intimately. God was tangibly near – the source of her joy and stability. She dedicated her life to seeking and serving Christ within her community, and this life felt rich and meaningful. She was on a sure path. Then events began to turn against her. Hadewijch had a daring poetic freedom in the expression of her encounter with God; a dangerous freedom in a time when accounts of direct experience of God outside the control of the Church tended to be held in suspicion. She was accused of false teaching, and this was followed by expulsion from her community. Hadewijch was left to work her way through life and to seek God alone, without the support of familiar friends. Worst of all, the sense of God's closeness to her faded; her prayer returned to her empty. She felt discarded, misunderstood and let down.

Searching for language to express her condition she fastened on the image of the hazel that sends out its catkins in the first days of the year, full of the promise of warmer days, only for the bitter cold of winter to reassert its grip. Long months of waiting will pass before the fruit is formed. Was the hazel's early flowering no more than foolishness – a deceit? Yet Hadewijch knew that a day was coming when the hazel would bear its fruit; after long months

---

2 Hadewijch texts are taken from: Mother Columba Hart O.S.B., 1980, *Hadewijch: the Complete Works,* translation and introduction by Mother Columba Hart, preface by Paul Monmaers, New York: Paulist Press. Abbreviations used in citing texts are: PS. (Poems in Stanza), PC. (Poems in Couplets), L. (Letters). This quotation is from PS. 17.

of waiting, what was begun would be completed. The seasons must take their course, and she must endure her present suffering as she had earlier enjoyed the riches of joy.

Hadewijch understood that as there are rhythms in the turning year, so there are rhythms in the course of outward events and within the world of feelings. Christ too, she thought, knew different seasons for: 'All his works had their time . . . and when the hour came he acted . . . in consolations, in miracles . . . in pains, in shame, in calumny, in anguish.'[3] It is a remarkable thought: Christ active for our salvation in vulnerable fear and in being in the power of those who would destroy him, every bit as much as in healing the sick or raising the dead. All these works had their time. Rain, drought, heat and cold all have their place within the turning year. Whilst one may awake joy and another sorrow, all belong. Times of pain, loss and struggle are painful and unwanted; yet they are no more a departure from what should be than times of happiness, growth and fullness. All have their hour. Hadewijch was not suggesting we should – even if we were able to – simply ride over our emotional responses, dismissing them as nothing. There is emotion in plenty in her letters and poetry. Christ's anguish and our anguish are very real and felt intensely, as is our laughter and exhilaration. When the winter wind comes from the east we feel its bitter cold, and when the sun breaks through the cloud on a June day we draw in its warmth. We learn to feel, but live through different seasons and come to understand they are part of a greater whole that underpins the rich natural rhythm of life.

Most of us have a favourite season. Mine is late spring, so full of growth, freshness and promise. Warmth is in the air and every tree unfurls its leaves in shades of green light. Day lingers invitingly; returning from work there is time in the evening to wander through the garden and see what has come up in my absence. I photosynthesize in the sun – or at least that's how it seems as new energy awakes within me. On the other hand, the most difficult of seasons for me is the slipping away of autumn into winter. I

3 L. 6

annually lament the clocks turning back, as if to throw in my face how short the days have become. Colour gives way to dull shades of grey and brown and I begin to feel enclosed by night; my mood at times as low as the midday sun in the sky.

The seasons of the earth have long been seen as a mirror of seasons of the heart. Spring is for 'spring-cleaning' – a time to shake off the dust and begin again. Everything is hopeful and possible. For many, winter is the season of 'our discontent',[4] with November its gloomy door:

No sun – no moon!
No morn – no noon –
No dawn – no dusk – no proper time of day . . .
No warmth, no cheerfulness, no healthful ease,
No comfortable feel in any member –
No shade, no shine, no butterflies, no bees,
No fruits, no flowers, no leaves, no birds –
November![5]

However, though there are times of year we naturally warm to and times that we endure, working on my allotment has helped me see the gift and necessity of each season, whether of the turning world or the changing experience of the heart. Seeds must fall to the ground and be broken open by rain and frost if they are to wake. Flowers fade away but even as they do so, their fruit prepares the way for a new generation. The soil needs winter rest and replenishment. Spent plants are uprooted and added to the compost heap; and there what seems lifeless and spent feeds future growth. There is a constant sense of movement in the garden with tasks to be done and a right day to do them: planting bulbs, pruning, feeding the soil, raking up leaves. There are times of rapid visible growth, and times of rest or dormancy. Gardeners have a habit of thinking a season

---

4 See the opening of Shakespeare's play *Richard III*
5 'November' by Thomas Hood, 1799–1845

ahead. I go out and dig on the bleakest of January days because I am conscious that a day will come when the sun will rise higher and stay longer, warming the soil so that it is fit for sowing. As dahlias, sunflowers and cosmos burst with colour on late summer days I wonder what bulbs to plant in autumn for a spring still further away.

So is there meaning and purpose in every season of our experience: in those times when what has been is falling away as much as when life seems to visibly expand and grow? Is there necessity in experiencing passages of time when, for all our effort, nothing seems to be moving on in ways we would describe as positive? Is there a rhythm in the patterning of events that we fail to perceive and live by? If we understood it a little more would we fret less and channel our energies more effectively? Within the natural world all the seasons form part of a larger cycle of growth; all have their necessary place. Might it also be so for us?

There is only one joy

Some 25 years ago I took part in a course for spiritual directors. At the heart of the experience was a guided 30-day retreat. Rest days, roughly once a week, punctuated the intensity of meeting oneself (and God) in the clarity of silence. These were times to walk, to sleep, to read something other than the Bible – whatever it took to take a deep breath before beginning again. On one such day in April the clouds rolled in from the hills bringing a cold rain that eventually turned to snow. Two of my fellow retreatants had very different reactions: one, from Scotland, turned her back to the window in her room, refusing to look out at this untimely outburst of winter. Another, from Malaysia, gazed in wonder at the miracle of snow. Hearing that her friend was so downcast she passed on a message: 'Tell her to look out of the window. There is only one joy.'

Last year, after the death of my father, the story came back to me. The years after retirement were perhaps the freest and most enjoyable my parents had known: holidays in the sun, morning coffee out in the town, their forming of a formidable if sometimes fractious badminton partnership. These were good times. As years went on the fabric of their lives gradually unwound. Physical problems became more dominant and then first my mother and then my father began to lose their minds to dementia. After my mother's death, my father seemed to rally for a while, digging out the jacket she had never let him wear. But daily life was precarious and after a series of falls he spent his last months in hospital. For long periods it seemed there was little breath of life left; but then he would sparkle again, telling us about his war years, or chatting up a nurse. And then he was gone.

It is tempting to cast these last years in terms of tragedy, compared with the flourishing of what had come before. They were certainly difficult times, not just for them, but for us as children who bore the anxiety and now feel the loss. But in me I hear someone telling me not to turn my back upon the experience but to gaze through the window, for 'there is only one joy'. Those painful, unsettling years held the gift of a new depth of intimacy with my father: holding and feeding him who had once held and fed me. In his stories, invited and repeated so many times, I saw his life afresh, not only as my parent but as a young man taking hold of the adventure the war years presented.

Like most people, I live in denial of growing older; I don't want to know. With two parents who developed dementia I wonder whether that will be my road too, and hope I won't be too embarrassing when I'm no longer in a state to wholly care! But having gazed through that window I am less afraid. If my father, through his dependence on others, could bring forth such love and knit together a family who, up to then, had lived too far apart, who am I to say that this happening to me would constitute a tragedy?

I am not in the land of easy answers, and I know there are far more difficult pains people bear than this. There are deaths where there is no time to say goodbye – no opportunity to speak the unsaid. But the thought remains that the unanticipated and unwanted sorrow, the messiness of fading health and increasing dependence on others, and the stark reality of death are yet part of the mysterious bundle of life. Such a belief takes us far from the prevailing spirit of our time, where wellbeing is defined by youth, beauty and vitality, as if there were but one good season in human existence.

I naturally see the beauty in the blue of a summer cornflower or the painted interior of the tulip bowl in spring, but it has taken more looking to see beauty in a brown autumn seed-head or lichen finding a home on a winter branch. But now I have seen it, like snow in April, I begin to know joy.

A time for everything

> For everything there is a season
> and a time for every matter under heaven;
> a time to be born and a time to die;
> a time to plant and a time to pluck up what is planted.[6]

This reflection from Ecclesiastes must be one of the most familiar of bible passages. Every movement of life and death has its fitting moment. The world turns and, willing or unwilling, we must turn with it. The Church in its pattern of recurring liturgical seasons echoes the same thought. We are invited to place ourselves in step with different and essential movements of the spiritual life. I am writing in Advent: a time of knowing our need of God and turning to him with joyful hope, waiting for the salvation God will bring. Whereas a secular Christmas arrives and goes as quickly as wrapping paper on a child's present, for the Church the weeks of Christmastide provide an invitation to continue pondering the mystery of God present with us and for us in the place where we are. The 40 days of Lent bid us turn away from what is harmful and self-diminishing and turn to Christ, the source of our life and wellbeing. Holy Week pitches us into the pain and confusion of suffering and death, only for us to be surprised again by the wonder of Easter resurrection. Like the natural seasons, we experience the changing colours of the Church's year again and again. It may seem like a fairground ride where we circle round

---

6 Ecclesiastes 3.1–2

and round, continually experiencing a difference in our perspective but without any substantial moving on: another carol service, and another Lent to consider doing without something we value. However, each time we celebrate these seasons we do so from a different place. The tree that greens in springtime is a different tree from the one reborn the previous year; it has put on new branches and sent out new roots. In the same way we will have had new experiences of how God is alongside us and within us, or face new situations where we need God's help to bring about renewal in our lives. If we are faithful in our search for God the cycle of seasons does more than lead us round in a circle to the same place: each cycle leads us more deeply into the mystery of our human existence and of God.

Each season, however, has its own notes; each bears a challenge and invitation. Hadewijch saw that whatever our years, every springtime reminds us that 'Love is ever new' and summons us to be 'born again' and to 'continual new acts of goodness'.[7] Our language echoes the call. Spring is a season, but it is also fresh water, ever-renewing itself, surfacing through hard rock. Spring is a coil of metal, carrying within itself the power once used to subdue it. Spring is a leap forward, beyond the circumspect, that dares to seek new ground. The word and the season bid us begin again and find through action powers of resilience and renewal that are, and are not, our own.

On the other hand, for Hadewijch, the fall of autumn leaves brought with it echoes of the call to renunciation. Not once, but over and again, we are to consent to let go by 'leaning on Love' and 'going where the beloved' leads.[8] There are times for letting go and accepting endings. It is alright in season not to be able to understand or shape events. We will grieve. And then a season comes that dares us to step out once more and take the risk of life and loving. Beyond fear or care we are to commit our all to what really matters. And then another season when what is needed is

7 PS. 7
8 PS. 7

not our movement but our stillness, not our activity, but our passivity to the work of God within.

The God of movement and stillness

Changes happen in our outer and inner worlds. Events unfold and ask new things of us. Is God the one and only firm fixture around which all else turns, or is there any sense in which God too is moving? Over the years I have seen how people look to the Church to be a refuge from a world where all else seems in flux: 'At least the Church will stay familiar, reliable, and predictable.' But it too moves on as it adapts to new contexts and challenges. Uncertainty and conflict can result from the movement of a piece of church furniture or the switch to a different hymnbook, let alone the larger matters of the place of women's ministry or attitudes to people of different sexual orientation! In one church I visited the times of church services had been carved in its solid stone walls by its nineteenth-century founders. It is a natural instinct. When Peter was captivated by the sight of Jesus, Moses and Elijah shining like the sun on the mountain of the Transfiguration he asked if he could build tents there for, he said, 'it is good for us to be here.'[9] We want to hold on to what feels safe and rewarding. In my early twenties I had it all worked out: God was with me, would see me through every difficulty and would heal every brokenness. But then a problem came that would not be resolved, and a hurt arose that would not heal, and in answer to my questions: 'why?' and 'why not?' there was only an obstinate silence. And yet this was also God, and I knew deep down, not a suddenly less loving or capable one.

I remember once having a picture of myself paddling in the shallowest waters of the sea and thinking how stupid it would be for me to suppose that I therefore knew all there was to know about it. Going deeper into the waves the sea becomes quite a different thing, and deeper still, something beyond anything I can ever know. For Hadewijch, God is 'Love'. Yet 'Love' is not one thing,

---

9 Matthew 17.4

at least in how we know her. One of her poems begins: 'Love has seven names: Chain, light, live coal and fire . . . dew, living spring, and hell.'[10] It seems the oddest of lists; yet it has its roots in experience. Take the thought that love is a 'chain'. Being in love and being loved is a wonderful thing; we know by this chain that 'there is no separation from Love' – our life is held secure. But on the other hand by this same bond we 'suffer the chains of Love': we feel our lover's separation from us most intensely. Love has the all-consuming nature of fire; we feel devoured by it, unable to focus on anything else. And yet love is also the gentle dew: the calm and peace bestowed on our troubled spirit by a lover's touch or a lover's word. Love is the living spring of our life – our deepest awakening. And yet Love may also be the hell of being 'forever in unrest' as we experience the discomfort of being called out of our niggardly ways into ever more generous self-gift. The poem describes how radically different the taste of this Love is in different seasons. 'Naught changeth thee' is in part true. There is a consistency in the shape of God's working, as acknowledged in the Christian Creed. God is ever creative, ever alongside, ever at work to heal and make free, continually drawing all being into unity. Yet we experience God in very different ways: alive and untameable, beyond any attempt at simple boxing in. God is the activity of love: a continual creativity at work in and through our lives. Jesus described the Spirit of God as ever-surprising movement: 'The wind blows where it chooses and you hear the sound of it, but you do not know where it comes from or where it goes.'[11] In another poem Hadewijch describes this paradoxical presence: the God who is forever still and moving, forever beyond our grasp:

> To lose one's way in her is to touch her close at hand;
> To die of hunger for her is to feed and taste
> Her despair is assurance
> Her sorest wounding is all curing

---

10 PC. 16
11 John 3.8

Wordlessness is her most beautiful utterance
Imprisonment by her is total release
Her deepest silence is her sublime song
Her wealth is the lack of everything
Her highest being drowns us in the depths.[12]

Our experience of God then may be seasonal in nature, known in many different weathers. This is 'Love' but not always in a form we recognize, know or find convenient.

I too, like Hadewijch, stop to look at hazel bushes. They are the most extraordinary 'ordinary' trees. If you study them in late summer you may see all seasons gathered together on a single branch. The broad green leaves of summer begin to colour for the autumn fall; the prized, long-awaited fruit is still ripening in clusters. Look more closely and you see the most delicate of catkins already beginning to form and the embryo buds of next year's growth. There is one symphony of life here but with its very different movements. At one time we might sense God's nearness and at another her apparent absence. Life seems full of blessing, and then events turn against us. Yet there are constancies within a changing world. For Hadewijch the most fundamental of these, despite all we might experience or feel, is the Love that is God, ever present to us and for us. Our constancy is invited in return: the ordering of life towards seeking and serving the Love who first seeks and serves us. Hadewijch understood that whatever happened, and no matter what turn her feelings took, her basic orientation as a human being must remain the same:

Let him whom Love has ever blessed
Be – according to the season of the year –
Sad or joyful
And always on Love's side.[13]

---

12 PC. 13
13 PS. 36

The Love that is God is present for us within the hardship of cold days, frozen ground and long nights as much as in birdsong, daffodils and sunshine; it is only that our feelings tell us otherwise. I can see growth taking place in April; I see decay in November; yet both times are integral to life.

Waiting on God

The changing seasons bid us to befriend waiting. Whether it is the first snowfall of winter or the first cuckoo call of spring we wait until the moment is given, not being able to bring it about by our own efforts, or even say: 'It will happen on such and such a day.' A rural society dependent on growing and gathering from the land is attuned to the necessity of waiting:

> Be patient, therefore, beloved, until the coming of the Lord. The farmer waits for the precious crop from the earth, being patient with it until it receives the early and the late rains. You also must be patient. Strengthen your hearts, for the coming of the Lord is near.[14]

Roots and fruits are received with thanksgiving when their time comes. Seed is sown in ground that has been prepared and nurtured, and sun and rain combine to bring about harvest in due season. There is work to be done, care to be taken, watchfulness to be maintained to ensure the moment is not lost. Yet growth itself is mysterious, never wholly in human hands, carrying for those who stop to perceive it a sense of wonder and gift:

> The Kingdom of God is as if someone would scatter seed on the ground, and would sleep and rise night and day, and the seed would sprout and grow; he does not know how. The earth produces of itself, first the stalk, then the head, then the full grain in the head. But when the grain is ripe, at once he goes in with his sickle, because the harvest has come.[15]

---

14 James 5.7–8
15 Mark 4.26–9

Urban society, however, is culturally estranged from waiting. Waiting is a form of curse: a breakdown of the system and a manifestation of inefficiency. It is what we do when things have gone wrong or don't work. We wait for the delayed train, the slow internet connection, the automated and uncaring customer 'care' line. Waiting is rarely a good. The urban world is built around speed. The great endeavour is saving time. The watchword is being in control and so not having to be dependent upon another. All falls apart when we're stuck in the traffic jam, more powerless to move forward than Moses before the waters of the Red Sea.

The Christian year begins not with the great feasts of Christmas, Easter or Pentecost but with waiting. Advent is in many ways a stark season – a time to be in touch with inner emptiness and need. It is a season of longing directed towards Christ, revealed as God-with-us, *Emmanuel*. The world begins not with an act but with a space: with the formless void that the Spirit hovers over, with the dust of the earth from which humankind will be formed, and with the sometimes painful recognition of our incompleteness. Advent is a season of waiting, but in hope and in expectation:

I wait for the Lord; my soul waits,
And in his word I hope.
My soul waits for the Lord
More than those who watch for the morning.[16]

The beginning is the meeting of our longing and God's generous giving. We do not make ourselves: we create the space for our making. Advent reminds us that everything is gift and that God goes on creating – if we only allow the room. Tiredness, restlessness, the inability to bring about meaningful change can become the open door to God if we turn that way. The beginning is not the act, but the waiting.

As the year begins, so it continues. Waiting remains at the heart of all that takes place. It is not that we are required to fold our

---

16 Psalm 130.5–6

hands and do nothing. This waiting is *active*. Life is in our hands. It is the one who seeks who finds, and the one who asks who receives, and the one who knocks who will find the door opened.[17] Whether we are seeking greater inner wholeness, a more purposeful way of living or a deeper rooting in God, our engagement is required. And yet the change we seek is never wholly in our power to bring about. It is God who 'makes things grow'.[18] In the end, everything is gift, even if the gift works through the work we do to receive it.

Sowing and harvest

> Those who go out weeping
> bearing the seed for sowing,
> shall come home with shouts of joy
> carrying their sheaves.[19]

It is often easier to make sense of difficult times as we look back on them. We see the fruit of them in our own growth or in greater understanding of others, even if we would never go out of our way to repeat the experience! What is done within one season makes possible what takes place within another. But often we cannot know this. We sow seeds in tears and it is difficult to believe they can bear any harvest. Each season has to be lived through on its own terms. There is, however, a further perspective to keep in mind. Our lives have meaning not only through personal achievement but in what they contribute to the common life we share.

On a winter day, sunlight is the more precious for being so brief. Walking around our local heath I glimpse sloes hung like jewels amongst the hedgerows. As the light fades, starlings sing an antiphon for the night. A thought comes: when my season ends I will still be part of everything. I am not thinking of a Christian heaven – whatever that might be – or the way my atoms will be reconstituted

---

17 Luke 11.9–10
18 1 Corinthians 3.5–9
19 Psalm 126.6

into new and living matter after my death. What comes to my mind is how other people have helped create me and how in some ways smaller or larger I have helped create them. Sometimes it is done in a moment, as this person's word or that person's action has entered into me and is now a part of who I am, integral to my story. Other relationships form us over long years as readily as a river helps shape its landscape. We leave our mark on one another, often without realization; and though this may sometimes be for harm still it is given us to be the bringers of life for one another. There are many such life-givers whose kindness or inspiration continues to wake in me. I always wanted to make some distinctive mark in my life; but maybe I have already done so and am unaware, just as others have unknowingly transformed me. We die, and we never really die.

For myself, I hope to live through many more seasons. The challenge for each of us is to meet every winter, spring, summer or autumn with all the openness and generosity we can. Hadewijch accepts suffering as part of life, an expected season, in a way in which people of our own age perhaps seek to avoid. To the question: 'Why?', so often on her own lips, she finds the answer: 'Why not?' Whatever the season, and whatever we experience, God is for us in friendship 'before all pain, and in all pain, and above all pain, and yes, beyond all pain.'[20]

For reflection:

1] What time is it?

Look at the passage below and think about what time it is in your life. You can choose a phrase from the poem or add one of your own.

> For everything there is a season,
> and a time for every matter under heaven:
> a time to be born, and a time to die;
> a time to plant, and a time to pluck up what is planted;

---

20 L. 28

a time to kill, and a time to heal;
a time to break down, and a time to build up;
a time to weep, and a time to laugh;
a time to mourn, and a time to dance;
a time to throw away stones, and a time to gather stones
together;
a time to embrace, and a time to refrain from embracing;
a time to seek, and a time to lose;
a time to keep, and a time to throw away;
a time to tear, and a time to sew;
a time to keep silence, and a time to speak;
a time for love, and a time for hate;
a time for war, and a time for peace.[21]

2] Listening to creation

Being attentive to the created world around us sensitizes us to the
passing of the seasons. In our life with God there will be seasons
too: time to act, and time to rest; time to change direction or try new
things; time to let go. Listening to, and watching the passing of times
and seasons can make us alive to what movement is needed in our life
in God. And so we ask not just: 'What do I need / want to do?', but also
'What is God doing in me and how can I co-operate with this?'

Go for a walk in a park or open space and notice the signs of the
seasons around you. If something catches your attention let it hold
your gaze. To gaze is to look in a focused but relaxed way. Look at
the colours, the shape and the structure. What do you see? Be open,
quiet and attentive without trying too hard to make something happen. How does what you look at speak to this season in your life?

3] What are you waiting for?

- For the next step on your path through life to become clear?
- For an answer to a question?

---

21 Ecclesiastes 3.1–8

- To become free within?
- To find purpose or peace in your life?
- For the fruit to come of what you have sown and nurtured?

Waiting is at the heart of prayer.

Wait now in the presence of the Lord.
Name before God what it is you are seeking.
Hold before God the desires of your heart — even those too deep
to name.
Let go to God, not in resignation but in hope.
Everything is gift, and God is generous in meeting our deepest
needs.
Ask God what it is you can do to help bring an answer to your
prayer.
But be content to wait . . .

4] The seasons in your life

What season(s) are you experiencing now? You may also recognize the
pattern of these seasons as you look back at your journey over time.

Autumn

- Where in your life do you sense the need to let go?
- Where do you sense a process of letting go already taking
place in your life?
- Some things have always deserved to be let go, for they are
lifeless and life-denying. Others have been valuable to you;
but is now the time to put them down and move on?

Winter

- Where in your life do you sense the need to 'let be', for now is
a time for waiting and resting?
- What in you is dormant, maybe feels stuck, but perhaps there
are the first stirrings of life here?

Spring

- What in you is springing to life or bubbling up from deep down inside?
- Where in your life do you sense energy – perhaps fleeting, faint and easy to miss?
- What new sense of direction do you begin to see taking shape within you?

Summer

- What feels alive, free, and fully formed within you?
- What within you do you long to share with others?
- Where do you see you are able to make a difference to others?

5] A winter prayer

For the rhythm of the seasons,
for drawing us deeper into your life,
for the bareness and clarity of winter days,
we praise you Lord.

For stillness and waiting,
for letting go and remembering our dependence,
for the passing of what has been,
we praise you Lord.

For new beginnings from dark places,
for buds on bare branches,
and for the first shoots of life,
we praise you Lord.

5

Falling Down

Across the centuries Julian of Norwich writes of a God who is gentle, courteous and intimately alongside us. Our life begins, continues and finds its fulfilment in love. Her best known words, quoted by the poet T.S. Eliot, are: 'All shall be well, and all manner of things shall be well.'[1] But how deep does this comfort run? What power does it have when faced with the muddle, mess and melancholy many of us face, or the sufferings endured by those we care for, or the evil carried out by human being on fellow human being? These questions were Julian's own, and ones she dwelt with over long years of conversation with God. How had humanity fallen into such depths of difficulty? Why did God allow such distress? And what was God's response?

The story of 'the Fall' is perhaps one of the best known in the Bible.[2] The cast is small: Adam, a man; Eve, a woman conjured from Adam's rib; God, the provider of the garden where they enjoyed the best of things; and a serpent, smooth in words but not to be trusted. The fruit of every tree in the garden is given freely by God for the man and woman to eat – all except one: the tree of the knowledge of good and evil; for to eat the fruit of this tree is to die. The serpent persuades Eve, and through Eve, Adam, to seize this one fruit not granted them, for then, the serpent promises, they will 'be like God'. The deed is done, the fruit taken and eaten, and a further cast member – fear – enters the garden. The man and woman hide away when they hear the Lord God walking

---

1 Used by T. S. Eliot in *Little Gidding, Four Quartets*
2 Genesis 2–3

at the time of the evening breeze. They realize their nakedness and try and cover it. God understands what has been done and confronts them. In shame the woman blames the man, and the man blames the serpent. The garden is lost; they are driven from its plenty into a land where survival will be won only by the sweat of their labour. Life will be painful; there will be division and conflict between their descendants and all shall return to the dust of the earth from which they were formed.

The account of the Fall goes back to an oral tradition some three thousand years old. I can imagine the story being told and retold around the evening campfire, its familiar lines shaped and coloured by its tellers. Through it successive generations came to understand why life is as it is. What if we work back from Eden to those people who wove the story? What do we glimpse of their world and how they made sense of it? It seems the garden of plenty was a dream vision far removed from their reality. They survived more than thrived in a harsh landscape, better suited for growing thistles and thorns than the crops that would reliably feed them. Sorrow was never far away; early death a commonplace. The recriminations between Eve, Adam and the serpent, and the temptation to eat the forbidden fruit and so be like God, suggest how a difficult environment was made worse by conflict between different individuals and groups struggling for power. And what of God? On the one hand we hear of a God who creates and provides, freely giving the fruit of every tree bar one and desiring that humanity will flourish. On the other, God is threatened by humanity's attempt to be equal, and punishes wrongdoing severely. Suffering and difficulty flow from humanity's own actions but also from God. There is no way back to the garden and it is God who bars the way.

It was a picture that people of Julian of Norwich's times could easily identify with. For the great majority of people, daily life was a struggle for survival. The plague arrived in England in 1348 when she was a young girl of six years. England was embroiled in a long and costly war with France that must be paid for in taxes. It was a time of social unrest with ordinary working people seeking freedom from the heavy duty of labour and produce owed to their lords. When Julian was about 40 anger at the imposition of the first Poll Tax, and pent-up desires for deliverance from the burden of forced service, led to the great outburst of the 'Peasant's Revolt'; it was brutally put down. Periodic failed harvests brought hardship and famine to most families. True, Norwich as a then major city and port, showed signs of its prosperity, with the building of great churches and fine houses for its wealthy traders and landlords; but where there is wealth there is poverty in its midst: beggars on street corners; the sick and displaced with nowhere to go.

And what of God? There was something of the same sense of ambiguity in popular understanding. The figure of the Crucified Christ featured large in art and devotional literature. Here God is alongside people in their suffering, sharing their burdens. God is not only the all-powerful creator but the vulnerable redeemer. And yet the Last Judgement was never far from view, vividly represented on church walls and brought into focus by every early death. Heaven – Eden – remained the subject of promise but hell, the punishment for sin, stood witness to God's wrath.

It might at first seem that the writings of a medieval anchoress[3] – a woman dedicated to a solitary life of prayer in a small dwelling attached to her local church – might have little to say about human suffering, whether of the people of her own time, or of lost Eden, or those of us who meet her writings today. She might seem separated not only by years but by the style of her life, seemingly removed from everyday concerns, pains and pressures. But in reality no question took up more of Julian's thought and prayer than hurting humankind. People came to her seeking counsel and help from God, leaving with her their worry, confusion and anguish. The long trail of human sorrow, the bewildering capacity of people to inflict suffering on others – all would have found a way to Julian's window. And like all of us, Julian would have had her personal losses, and had to deal with her own weakness and fallibility. She was not one who could easily

---

3 A helpful background to Julian's life and writings is provided by Grace Jantzen's *Julian of Norwich*, 2000, London: SPCK

brush aside what she heard, saw and felt. Her doubts surfaced nakedly in conversation with God. She was deeply troubled by sin, not just in the sense of wrongdoing but all the bodily and spiritual suffering that in some way flowed from it. As a loyal daughter of the Church she understood that all this unhappiness flowed from Adam's fall, and that through Christ's death and resurrection humanity had been rescued from the power of sin and given hope of new life; but she questioned why God had allowed it to happen in the first place. If God could foresee the damage human weakness would cause, why was 'the beginning of sin . . . not prevented?' For then, she mused, 'all would have been well.'[4] She sensed Jesus answering her:

> Sin is necessary, but all will be well, and all will be well, and every kind of thing will be well . . . it is true that sin is the cause of all this pain, but all will be well, and all will be well, and every kind of thing will be well.[5]

Julian is only partly reassured. She understands that in Christ's Passion God shares our deepest darkness and pain, and in his rising all that is broken will be made whole, but in the face of particular suffering she encounters through those she listens to and in news of events in the wider world, she struggles to see how any benefit can emerge or any meaning be found, for: 'There are many deeds which in our eyes are so evilly done and lead to such great harms that it seems impossible that any good result could ever come of them.'[6] This feels a very modern observation. Our world feels so impossibly out of sorts, with individual people caught in the whirlwind of forces beyond their control: searing inequalities of poverty and

---

4 Unless otherwise indicated, all Julian of Norwich references indicate chapter numbers in the 'Long Text' in: Edmund Colledge and James Walsh, 1978, *Julian of Norwich: Showings*, translated and introduced by Edmund Colledge and James Walsh, New Jersey: Paulist Press

5 27

6 32

extreme wealth, fruitless and bloody conflicts, and the abuse of those who are most vulnerable. With Julian we might find ourselves 'contemplating it generally, darkly and mournfully' finding it hard to trace human good or divine redemption at work.[7] Julian is unable to be at rest with simple words of reassurance, questioning: 'Ah, good Lord, how could all things be well, because of the great harm which has come through sin to your creatures?'[8]

She receives no absolute answer. What she does see, and believes in passionately, is the costly, generous love of God expressed in Christ entering our sufferings, and the ultimate overcoming of evil and death in his resurrection. God provides neither explanation, nor visible resolution of troubles, but only this redemptive presence. At one point Julian wants a specific answer from God in relation to someone she loves and cares for.[9] However, she finds that her need to be certain of this impedes her trust that *all* are kept in the mercy and grace of God. It is as if our desire to have specific answers (*show me why this has happened and how it will turn for good*) stands in the way of the growth of larger hope and trust in the goodness and resourcefulness of God's working (*I can't see how this can work out but I let go into your love*). Yet for all that she cannot see, Julian is assured that the love of God is not mere words or talk, nor something so general that it has no room for the particular:

> He wants us to know that he takes heed not only of things that are noble and great, but also those which are little and small, of humble men and simple, of this man and that man . . . Every kind of thing will be well.
> . . . Just as the Blessed Trinity created all things from nothing, just so will the same blessed Trinity make everything well which is not well.[10]

---

7 29
8 29
9 35
10 32

But then another layer of questioning enters Julian's conversation with God: how to reconcile the Church's teaching that because of the sin of Adam all people are subject to sin and therefore deserving of punishment, and her own perception of being unable to see any blame put upon us by God: no anger, and no desire to inflict pain:

> And one article of faith is that many creatures will be damned . . . all these will be eternally condemned to hell, as Holy Church teaches me to believe. And all this being so, it seemed to me that it was impossible that every kind of thing should be well.[11]

Here we see Julian in conflict. She wants to be true to the teaching of the Church and of the Scriptures. Yet she instinctively rejects the violent measure of justice in her day, when in her own city people were put to death for their beliefs or because they dared stand up against oppressive landlords. Julian finds in her own heart no desire to punish people for wrongdoing; rather she sees the inner confusion and unhappiness from which their destructiveness springs. Everything she has experienced leads her to know God as unending compassion; one who labours to create and give being and not to destroy:

> In all this contemplation it seemed to me that it was necessary to see and to know that we are sinners and commit many evil deeds which we ought to forsake, and leave many deeds undone which we ought to do, so that we deserve pain, blame and wrath. And despite all this, I saw truly that our Lord was never angry, and never will be. Because he is God, he is good, he is truth, he is love, he is peace; and his power, his wisdom and his charity do not allow him to be angry.[12]

The focal point of Julian's contemplation of God was always Christ on the cross. What does she see there? God does not respond to

---

11 32
12 46

the mess, harm and cruelty worked by humanity by throwing them aside, or inflicting punishment. Instead Christ vulnerably and generously comes alongside us, bearing in his own body our pains – and all to comfort us and free us from the harm we do one another and know no way out of. The desire to punish and blame has no root in God; rather it is a symptom of our estrangement:

> For I saw no wrath except on man's side, and he forgives that in us, for wrath is nothing else but a perversity and an opposition to peace and to love. And it comes from a lack of power or a lack of wisdom or a lack of goodness, and this lack is not in God but it is on our side.[13]

So Julian wrestles to reconcile what will not fit: a God of endless and active compassion and the Church's teaching on punishment due to sin: 'Between these two oppositions my reason was greatly afflicted by my blindness and I could have no rest.'[14] It is at this point that Julian's attention is brought back by God to a picture she received many years before, a 'wonderful example of a lord who has a servant.'[15]

The Lord and Servant[16]

Following Julian's line of reflection and questioning what do we have so far? Everything that Julian experienced led her to understand that God is always the activity of love: coming alongside us in our muddle and our sorrow, and there creatively drawing us into life and being. She understands 'sin' to be the root of human pain but not in any way because of a desire within God to punish for wrongdoing. She accepts what the Church teaches about hell but cannot bring herself

---

13 48

14 50

15 51

16 The quotations in this section on the Lord and Servant are taken from: Elizabeth Spearing, 1998, *Julian of Norwich, Revelations of Divine Love (Short Text and Long Text)*, London: Penguin Books.

to believe a compassionate God would ever desire to leave one who is loved within such a place. And in answer to her search to resolve the tensions between her loyalty to the teaching of the Church and her conviction of an ever-merciful God she receives an illustration that centres on the relationship between a lord and servant.

In Julian's first account of her experiences and their meaning, – the 'Short Text' written when she was in her early thirties – the story of the lord and servant does not appear. She pondered the image granted her at that time but could make no meaningful sense of it and so put it aside. But twenty years later it became the centre-point of the 'Long Text' – the fruit that fell from the tree of her steadfast enquiry. She drew back into her memory the picture once given her:

> The first kind of vision was this: the bodily likeness of two people, a lord and a servant . . . The lord looks at the servant lovingly and kindly, and he gently sends him to a certain place to do his will. The servant does not just walk, but leaps forward and runs in great haste, in loving anxiety to do his lord's will. And he falls immediately into a slough and is very badly hurt. And then he groans and moans and wails and writhes, but he cannot get up to help himself in any way. And in all this I saw that his greatest trouble was lack of help, for he could not turn his face to look at his loving lord, who was very close to him, and who is the source of all help; and like a man who was weak and foolish for the time being, he paid attention to his own senses, and his misery continued . . . His reason was blinded and his mind stunned to such an extent that he had almost forgotten his own love for the lord . . . He lay alone; I looked hard all around, and far and near, high and low, I could see no one to help him . . . the place where he lay was long, hard and full of difficulties.[17]

Initially Julian understands the servant to be Adam, and for her Adam is everyone; she is Adam, the person whose sorrows she

---

17 51, p. 115–16

listens to is Adam, as is the warlord who kills innocent people for the sake of his cause. When Adam falls he is thrown into confusion. He can no longer see the lord who loves him, or know who he is in the sight of that love. He despairs of himself and his misfortune, blindly striking out, now hurting himself, now wanting to inflict hurt on others. This is Julian's understanding of sin and its impact; it is a profound, painful and paralysing disorientation:

> The lord . . . I understood to be God. The servant who stood in front of the lord, I understood that he represented Adam, that is to say, that one man and his fall were shown in that vision to make it understood how God considers any man and his fall; for in the sight of God all men are one. This man's strength was broken and enfeebled, and his understanding was numbed, for he turned away from looking at his lord.[18]

She considers the way the lord looks on his servant, and sees there no desire to blame but rather compassion. Our falling brings as a consequence pain and distress but this is no punishment; instead, 'our kind Lord comforts and grieves . . . loving and longing to bring us to bliss.'[19] In terms reminiscent of the father of the 'prodigal son', Julian sees God taken up with concern for lost, hurting humankind:

> The place where our Lord sat was humble, on the barren earth, deserted, alone in a wilderness . . . his eyes were black, most comely and handsome, appearing full of tender pity, and within him there was a great refuge, long and wide and full of the endless heavens. And his tender expression as he kept looking at his servant, especially when he fell, I thought it could melt our hearts with love and break them in two with joy . . . The merciful gaze of his tender expression filled the whole earth and went down with Adam into hell; and this unending pity kept Adam from everlasting death. And this mercy and pity remain with

---

18 51, p. 118
19 51, p. 118

mankind until the time we come up into heaven. But man is blind in this life, and therefore we cannot see our Father, God, as he is . . . But his sitting on the barren earth in a deserted place means this . . . our kind Father would prepare no other place for himself, but sit upon the earth, waiting for mankind.[20]

But 'waiting' is not enough. As Julian continues to contemplate the picture of the lord and servant, another layer of meaning breaks through. The servant is not only Adam/everyone but also Christ. In a moment of time Christ falls into human flesh. And through this moment Christ transcends time, sharing every human journey and making his own every human pain.

When Adam fell, God's son fell; because of the true union made in heaven, God's son could not leave Adam . . . Adam fell from life to death into the valley of this wretched world, and after that into hell. God's son fell with Adam into the valley of the Virgin's womb . . . in order to free Adam from guilt in heaven and on earth; and with his great power he fetched him out of hell.[21]

Christ's willing fall into the depths of our difficulty – our failures, our fears and our frailties – provides a means of rising from the ground. And all the ways in which we account ourselves to be no one and nothing, not understanding who we are, begin to be overturned. We live in an everlasting Easter day where the most beautiful and unexpected rising is our own:

The body was in the grave until Easter morning, and from that time he lay down no more; for then was truly ended the tossing and turning, the groaning and moaning; and our foul mortal flesh which God's son took upon himself, which was Adam's old tunic, tight, bare and short, was then made by our Saviour newly beautiful.[22]

20 51, p.118–19
21 51, p. 121
22 51, p. 124

The lord and the servant is a beautiful picture, well worth pondering – its riches not grasped in a single reading. It leaves us with a picture of lost humankind, no longer knowing who we are because we do not see ourselves as God sees us. It presents an image of God's everlasting waiting and working to restore us to the beauty of our making, a truth and reality that is never lost. We see the humility and costly vulnerability of God's love, expressed in the Father's waiting on the bare earth and the Son's identification with humankind in all sorrow and joy. And significantly the story of the Fall is retold, this time seen not through human eyes but through the loving gaze of God. Though allowed to fall we have never been let go. God is revealed as the activity of love, ever alongside, ever creative, ever at work to make us whole. Adam is everyone, and so this parable is of the here, now and the particular: you are the one held in the Lord's unceasing gaze, and I am too; Christ chooses to fall into the depths of your difficulties, and into the struggles I experience within myself today.

And yet there are questions that remain. We still have no clear answer as to why humankind is allowed to fall in the first place. Julian's assertion that she sees no anger in God seems to go against the evidence – not least the angry Jesus causing chaos in the Temple as he drives out the moneylenders. Most importantly, what are the practical implications of this reworking of the story of the Fall for the way we see ourselves, and for how we allow God to draw us into wholeness?

Why is humankind allowed to fall in the first place?

Sin is necessary, but all will be well.[23]

The understanding that sin is 'necessary' – or in Julian's own word 'behovely' – follows a line of thought consistent in Christian

23 Colledge and Walsh, 1978, *Showings*, Chapter 27

literature, from Paul, through Augustine and on to Julian's times. The ancient Easter hymn, the *Exsultet*, celebrates Christ's intervention in these words:

> O happy fault
> O necessary sin of Adam
> That gained for us so great a Redeemer.

The sense is that Adam's fall, and all that flows from it in terms of human unease, opens the way for us to understand how deeply we are loved. Not that God sets us up to fall so that he might rescue us, as if we were a plaything. But that the circumstances of our falling – be it the fruit of our own actions or the unanticipated impact of events over which we had no control – allow us to comprehend how the Love that is God comes alongside us unconditionally, and at the greatest cost, and always gladly. Christ on the cross is not a symbol of might in any human terms, but the expression in action of divine love, so powerful and so deep that it asks no questions of whether you or I deserve it or whether it is wise to give so much.

Why does God not intervene to prevent unhappiness and wrongdoing? Julian consistently affirms the 'courtesy' of God. Within God there is no desire to dominate his creation or to manipulate our responses. Instead God grants us independence of choice. Such freedom allows our falling and this is the risk God consents to make. We trace something of the same pattern within our own experience. There is a troubling process of letting go involved in parenting, or in schooling someone in a new skill. If a child is to grow up he or she must progressively be set free to do things their way and learn through the pain of getting things wrong. The day comes when the apprentice has to be given responsibility, and the results will not always be good. Love does not allow us to micromanage the lives of others. We might keep them safe but at the cost of stunting their development and boxing in their individuality.

Yet whilst the love of God is expressed in letting go, the same love is expressed in coming alongside us in all humility and vulnerability to be the means of our integration. The incarnation is not an afterthought of God to put right what is broken; it is an expression within time of the eternal and active desire of God that despite everything, all *will* be well. Not all our suffering, or even most of it, is the fruit of our own actions; we are 'done to' as much as we 'do'. But then Julian does not believe that there exists any direct line between this person's pain and their wrongdoing, as would be the case were suffering punishment for wrongdoing. It is Adam, everyone, who is ill at ease, hurt and hurting, trapped in the ditch; but everyone is also Christ, rising from the tomb of suffering, whether 'deserved' or 'undeserved'.

No anger in God

I saw truly that our Lord was never angry, and never will be.[24]

Perhaps there is nothing that Julian says that is so bold, so startling and so challenging than her assertion that anger does not belong to God. In this statement she undermines the religious framework of her time with its system of indulgences to limit punishment due to sin, graphic visual depictions of hell and merciless treatment of heretics. By implication, this is more projection of human disintegration than expression of divine will.

'No anger in God' might sit uneasily in our time for another reason: it suggests divine indifference. There were, and there are, things to be angry about: injustice, the exploitation of the vulnerable, the casual misuse of the earth's resources or the violent pursuit of power. And indeed there are times in the Gospels when Jesus *is* angry; he overturns the tables of those exploiting the poor in the Temple, and he confronts those who use the God-given Law as a weapon against people. Anger is part of our human identity. There are times when we can use our anger positively to overcome the fear that holds us back from doing what is right and life-giving. Anger can be energy *for* life.

---

24 46

So what is Julian expressing when she says that she sees no anger in God? Julian believes passionately that God does not punish or blame, for the very desire to punish or blame is, in her understanding, wholly opposed to who God is. Rather than seeking retribution, or remaining aloof and indifferent, Julian sees God as enduringly creative, incarnate and redemptive, vulnerably entering our places of pain, bringing not only forgiveness but seeds of transformation. There is no anger in God in the sense of anything that is destructive, or that seeks to discard and to distance, or that desires to burden and diminish the other. If there is anger in God, it is anger for life that works against all that deforms and devalues. It looks reality in the face and finds against the odds something beautiful there, something worth living and dying for. It is justice expressed as mercy – always as mercy.

Sin is nothing

Our personal failures are perhaps as hard as any falls to bear. The gap between the life we aspire to and the life we live can be a wide and painful one. Why do we hurt those we love and who love us? Why do we casually spoil and waste the riches we have received? Why do we come to the same place again and again, face to face with the weakness of our resolution to do things differently? We are often our harshest critics, passing judgement not only on our offence but on the nature and character of the offender. There are times when we see no good in us and find little ground for self-belief. Yet Julian claims that God's goodness 'fills all his creatures and all his blessed works full, and endlessly overflows in them.'[25] What is the true: our sorrowful estimation of our own worth, for which we can readily find evidence, or Julian's vision of the overflowing goodness of God expressed in our being? Julian says something startling, that sin is nothing:

---

25 5

84

O wretched sin, what are you? You are nothing. For I saw God is in everything; I did not see you. And when I saw that God has made everything, I did not see you . . . And when I saw that God does everything that is done, the less and the greater, I did not see you. And when I saw our Lord Jesus Christ seated in our soul so honourably, and love and delight and rule and guard all that he has made, I did not see you. And so I am certain that you are nothing.[26]

Julian seems preoccupied with sin in the sense of the harm and disorder humankind endures and brings about, so there can be no way that she is simply ignoring its significance or impact. Rather, she understands that sin is 'no-thing' because it does not flow from God who is the *being* of all living things. It is a distortion of the real and true – a destructive denial of the overflowing and ever-creative life of God.

I remember going to a hall of mirrors. Each gave me a different version of myself: now giraffe tall, now a squat and round dumpling. Because I looked in other mirrors that reflected more truly, I could laugh at what I saw. But what if the only mirrors I had available were distorted in such ways? Might I begin to believe what I saw, and then act from that belief? For Julian, the true mirror is found in relationship with God in whose image and likeness we are made. Julian's servant no longer knew who he was because he had lost sight of the lord who loved him and was so close to him. He struck out, confused and hurting. We do not know who we are, for we do not see our truth reflected in the eyes of God. What is it that God sees? This is the true mirror. I am continually struck by what happened when Jesus looked at people who felt themselves to be nothing and no one and behaved accordingly. The hated tax collector Zacchaeus welcomes Jesus to his house. The woman of Samaria leaves her water jar at the well, so overcome is she by the impact of her meeting with a stranger who asked her for a drink. When they met his gaze, and discovered not ridicule or condemnation, but the surprise of being known

---

26 Colledge and Walsh 1978, *Showings*, Short text: chapter xxxiii

and understood, they visibly rose from the ditch of their self-disregard. What they saw, and what we might see if we follow the line of their gaze, is not only the Lover but what is loved. It is you, it is I.

The wrong we do does not flow from some hidden evil core but from the confusion and disorientation that makes us unable to see who we really are. We choose what is destructive and false, bringing harm on one another and upon ourselves. But we are, and always will be, created in the image of God. This is the real and the true, the being that flows from the love and goodness of God, and the being that God endlessly works to bring forth. The remedy lies in placing ourselves within the relationship we are made for in the depths of our being. We can only know our deepest self – what Julian calls our 'soul' – by seeing ourselves as God sees us. In seeking God we find ourselves:

> For our soul sits in God its true rest, and our soul stands in God in sure strength, and our soul is naturally rooted in God, in endless love. And therefore if we want to have knowledge of our soul . . . we must seek in our Lord God in whom it is enclosed.[27]

Contrition, compassion and longing for God

For Julian contrition, compassion and sincere longing for God are the 'medicines' that enable us to move along a path towards wholeness. She also describes them as 'wounds'.[28] The term is carefully chosen. We are wounded by our falling, but these very pains can move us towards wholeness. The risen Christ still shows the marks of his wounds, but whereas once these marked great harm, now they have become the source of our healing.

Falling is painful. I see again I am not able to think or behave as I wish to do. I lack the commitment and resolution to continue along the path that I know is life-giving. I experience my lack of

27 56
28 39

integration. My illusion of self-sufficiency crashes to the ground. But I understand again how much I need God and just how confused and destructive I can become without this anchor. I turn again to look at God and let God look at me. Contrition draws us back to where life is. It expresses self-awareness and humility. However Julian does not advise that we become self-absorbed, drowning in our own misery. That way only leaves us in the ditch, feeling alone and worthless, thoroughly stuck in the mire of our misery. Instead we look at God, contemplating with wonder and gratitude the love in which we continue to be held. This helps us rise up and move forward:

> Our courteous Lord does not want his servants to despair because they fall often and grievously; for our falling does not hinder him in loving us.[29]
>
> And here I understood that the Lord looked on the servant with pity and not with blame; for this passing life does not require us to live wholly without sin. He loves us endlessly, and we sin customarily, and he reveals it to us most gently. And then we sorrow and moan discreetly, turning to contemplate his mercy, cleaving to his love and goodness, seeing that his is our medicine, knowing that we only sin.[30]

Contrition creates the space for the birth of compassion. As we gaze at God, choosing to give all for us, desiring to console us in our sorrow rather than blame us for our wrongdoing, so our own capacity for generous, merciful love grows. We begin to be able to forgive ourselves and forgive others. In allowing God to love us as we are, we slowly come to see what we cannot now see because of our blindness: the beauty and gift at the heart of the muddle human beings can be. By the working of 'mercy and grace' we are made 'fair and spotless'. Christ wishes us to be like him in 'undiminished, everlasting love towards ourselves and our fellow Christians.'[31]

---

29 39
30 82
31 40 For Julian 'our fellow Christians' is shorthand for 'everyone'.

The third wound is 'sincere longing for God'. In falling to the ground we remember afresh how God is the one and only foundation for our lives. It is where we belong and where we know who we are. Longing is the witness to God's Spirit within, drawing us into deeper relationship. A life shaped by longing for God, with space given to attentive openness to God in prayer, allows peace and love to be at work within us drawing us into wholeness:

Peace and love are always in us, living and working, but we are not always in peace and in love; but he wants us to take heed that he is the foundation of our whole life in love.[32]

We are not to be complacent, but we are not to beat ourselves up. Self absorption will lead us only deeper into the ditch, confused and alone.

Trusting in the constancy of God

We will continue to fall painfully to the ground. Sometimes this falling will be because of our actions: we fall short of what we aspire to be. At other times events beyond our control make us lose our balance and spiral downwards. And there will be many days when we experience the discomfort of the rise and fall of our feelings: now trusting, and now doubting; now at peace, and now full of anxiety and sorrow.

Julian describes such a day. She begins it feeling 'wholly at peace, at ease and at rest' believing nothing on earth can disturb her. But just moments later her assurance lies in ruins: 'I was changed and abandoned to myself, oppressed and weary . . . so that I hardly had the patience to go on living.' At one moment, she muses, 'I could have said with St. Paul: "Nothing shall separate me from the love of Christ", and in the next, with St. Peter, "Lord, save me for I am perishing."'[33]

---

32 39
33 15

Julian had a sense of humour, and we might need one too to deal with our own see-saw from Paul to Peter and hopefully back to Paul. But there is a constancy in which we can rest, and this lies in God, ever active in love for us, whatever we experience or feel, for 'God wishes us to know that he keeps us safe all the time, in sorrow and in joy . . . and both are one love.'[34] We hold within us fallen Adam and risen Christ, and if sometimes we live within one of these, the other is not lost to us:

> During our lifetime here we have in us a marvellous mixture of both well-being and woe. We have in us our risen Lord Jesus Christ, and we have in us the wretchedness and harm of Adam's falling . . . And we are so afflicted in our feelings by Adam's falling . . . but we wait for God, and trust faithfully to have mercy and grace; and this is his own working in us . . . and now we are raised to the one, and now we are permitted to fall to the other.[35]

God's constancy invites our constancy. This stability is not to do with our moods which swing this way and that with the turn of events. We will be happy and sad; we will see everything clearly and then be thrown into confusion so we seem to understand nothing at all. But gradually we come to recognize a resting place deeper than this moment, this feeling, even this failure. We choose to turn inwardly towards God, knowing our need; understanding that this love is the source of everything we are and will be. Falling down hurts, but Christ has fallen too, freely and gladly, and in him we shall rise. For Adam – everyone – all will be well:

> And these words: You will not be overcome, were said very insistently and strongly, for certainty and strength against every tribulation which may come. He did not say: You will not be troubled, you will not be belaboured, you will not be disquieted; but he said: You will not be overcome.[36]

---

34 15
35 52
36 68

For reflection:

1] Julian calls God our 'rest'. When we carry the burden of our failings, or of a situation that we cannot reconcile, it can help to physically rest our pain or our concern with God. Place a candle or cross somewhere in your home to symbolize your resting place in God. As something unresolved comes to mind place a stone, representing your burden, in your resting place and leave it there.

2] Use the sentences from Julian of Norwich below to lead you into prayer.[37] Read each one in turn, leaving quiet space between them to take into yourself their meaning, and their significance for you. You don't have to use all the sentences; if one holds your attention, stay with it. End by using Julian's prayer 'God, of your goodness . . .'

The highest form of prayer is to the goodness of God, which comes down to us in our humblest needs

He is the goodness of everything

He does not despise what he has made

He is our clothing,
who wraps and enfolds us for love,
embraces us and shelters us,
surrounds us for his love,
which is so tender that he may never desert us.

He is true rest

God, of your goodness, give me yourself
For you are enough for me,

---

37 Quotations are taken from Chapters 5 and 6 (Long Text) in Colledge and Walsh, 1978, *Showings*.

and I can ask for nothing which is less
which can pay you full worship.
And if I ask anything which is less,
always I am in want;
but only in you do I have everything.

6

A Way in the Wilderness

Guide me, O thou great Jehovah,
pilgrim through this barren land.
I am weak, but thou art mighty;
hold me with thy powerful hand.
Bread of heaven, bread of heaven,
feed me till I want no more;
feed me till I want no more.[1]

William Williams' great hymn of pilgrimage to the tune of *Cwm Rhondda* is one that gets everyone singing, whether in a church or a rugby stadium. There is no need for delicacy or worry about tunefulness; this one you can sing from the heart. The melody is rousing with its crescendo of a chorus but there is something about the words that connect too. Life is difficult and we do not know how things will work out; we are on our own and at the limit of our resources. We cry out for what we need to carry on: someone to feed, hold and guide us; someone to see us through.

Williams sums up in a few brief lines what a lifetime of experience confirms: we live on the edge of the unknown. When I was a student I inherited a wall poster from my room's previous occupant: 'Life is a journey, not a destination.' It sounded so magisterial, as if coming from one who held all the answers. Gazing at it day by day, what it awoke in me were questions:

---

1 Composed by William Williams, 1717–1791; translated from the Welsh by Peter Williams and the author.

'But doesn't the destination matter too? Where am I going, and why here and not there? What's the next step? Will I be able to cope?' For Williams the biblical exodus of the Israelites from the hands of their oppressors in Egypt, and their 40-year progress through the wilderness to a land flowing with milk and honey, was a metaphor for life's uncertainties. We are shaken in doubt and fear as we are led through experiences we can neither understand nor control; but we *are* led, and though we feel alone a provider keeps us company. Our frailty invites us to place our hope in one who holds us with a powerful hand. But if the hymn expresses confidence in God, anxiety is not far away. This pilgrim knows himself to be weak, lost and isolated. The wilderness is never an easy place to be.

For the Israelites the drama of liberation gave way to long years of wandering. The wilderness proved to be a place of testing and purification; an empty and vast wasteland without paths or ways. The Israelites' daily existence was precarious, supported only by God's gifts of water from the rock and manna from the sky. All efforts to store food and so be independent of outside help failed. The manna was decisively *daily* bread; each morning brought a new supply, but anything saved in case it should fail to arrive became worm-ridden or melted away. After the initial euphoria of escape the lack of any clear progress began to gnaw away confidence. Doubts and murmurings against Moses and his mysterious cloud-dwelling god grew louder with each day's failure to arrive at their destination. Kicking out against this seemingly endless and meaningless meandering, the people made an idol of a golden calf that they hoped would be more amenable to their bidding. And who could blame them? They had exchanged their bondage to slave-drivers for dependence on a provider they could neither see, nor understand, and who brought them no nearer to a land they could settle in.

But the journey did have meaning, and not just to do with the day they entered the Promised Land. Through their wanderings, a group of cowed and diminished slaves grew into their identity as the People of God. Though it took but a brief moment to deliver them from their outward oppressors, it took a generation to become free in mind. Trust opened the way to the liberty they had long sought, expressed in a covenant with Yahweh, the '*I AM*' who had kept them on their journey so that their feet had not swollen, nor the clothes on their back worn out.[2] The story is echoed in Jesus' temptations in the wilderness. The dramatic manifestation of God's presence at his baptism is followed by his being driven into the desert by the Spirit to be tested. Forty long days and nights pass. What idols or what God will he follow? What food will he eat? He too chooses to live not by bread alone but by every word that comes from the mouth of God.[3]

From the viewing-point of history, the wilderness experience was the place of revelation, the privileged time of formation. But for those who endured it, the wilderness was an in-between time, an interruption, a breakdown in the expected flow of events. Something was ended, yet lingered in the memory; something unknown was yet to be realized. Travelling, they had no more than vague hints of where their journey might take them. The only signposts in the desert are question marks.

What about us? Where does the wilderness lie? Where might we find it? Not only in sand and rock. It stretches between ending and beginning; between loss of meaning and its recovery; between awareness of deep longing and finding that which we long for; between questioning and the start of understanding. What makes it wilderness is that we do not know whether beginning *does* lie beyond ending. Is there meaning, or finding, or understanding? We hope for these things and might receive assurances of their existence but for now they are beyond reach not only of our physical grasp but of our imagination:

'How will I begin again now the partner I have built my life around has gone from me?'

---

2 Deuteronomy 8.4
3 Matthew 4.4

'When will I find the freedom to live my own life rather than a life other people have mapped out for me?'

'Now that the work that I put so much of myself into has been taken from my hands, what is there to live for?'

'I feel a sense of calling to this role but the doors are all closed to me, so what do I do now?'

'My ill health hangs over me like a dark cloud; how can I find a way of living positively again?'

'There is something more I want to do with my life but I don't seem to get anywhere.'

We have left one room and are moving on looking for the door that opens on to another; but for this time we are in a corridor. This is not a place that entices us to sit down and make a home; it is somewhere we must walk through. There are no windows to look out from that we might measure progress by. Is it going anywhere at all? Led down this turn and that turn we begin to wonder whether we are not doubling back on ourselves. Are we lost? Even turning back is denied to us; would we ever find the way? In any case we heard the door closing behind us and we have no way of opening it again. No, we can do no more than move on. But are we going anywhere? Where have all the signs gone just at the point when they are most needed? The corridor leads on; its length is measured not in metres but in days and weeks and years. But being a corridor it must lead somewhere – mustn't it?

Testing of the heart

The Gospel of Mark sums up Jesus' time in the desert in stark simplicity. No sooner had Jesus heard his Father in heaven assure him, 'You are my Son, the beloved, with you I am well pleased', than he found all such intimacy taken away:

And the Spirit immediately drove him out into the wilderness. He was in the wilderness for forty days, tempted by Satan; and he was with the wild beasts; and the angels waited on him.[4]

Matthew and Luke describe how Jesus is *led* into the wilderness; but for Mark Jesus is *driven*; choice is taken away. What does he experience there? A vast and empty landscape; no crowds; no one who needs him; no one to reflect back who he is. He is alone, and alone he must take this journey; but for how long, and for what purpose and for what outcome? Our hindsight knows, but he cannot. The past is a vivid memory but a lost country; there can be no return to his former village life with its trades and familiar company. The future is as featureless in certainty as this landscape. The cravings of his physical and emotional needs are as unrestrained as wild beasts: thirst, insecurity, loneliness, fear; they gather in hungry packs. Temptation lingers in the mind: to be no more than these feelings; to do no more than find some way to be delivered from them. Yet he *is* more; there *is* meaning and future though for now he cannot make out their shape. Unperceived the angels are with him; he is still the beloved to be watched over and defended; and though now he hears no voice of affirmation he remembers its sound and trusts himself to its provision. He endures. Emerging from the wilderness he has met himself. He knows what might ensnare him and where freedom lies. He is ready.

Are we led into the wilderness or are we driven, or is it sometimes both of these? I listen to different people tell their tale: a man who stumbles through grief for the partner he has lost, not knowing how, when, or if some stability to his life will return; a woman moved by disillusionment with the pattern of her life to set out in search of meaning, but who now mourns the security of what she had. His path is thrust unwillingly upon him, yet some inner resilience leads him to walk it. She chooses to let go of what fails to satisfy, yet as she walks finds she has gone beyond the

---

4 Mark 1.12–13

place where she can be in total control. For both the landscape is unfamiliar and the destination beyond imagining. It could be said that both move within a process. Grief is a way we work through loss to recover the possibility of meaningful and stable living without the one we mourn. We do not 'get over' the loss because there can be no return to a past existence; that has gone now, and the basis for a new one must be found. The person who is moved by dissatisfaction to set her life in a new direction may glimpse some way in which her future life will be framed, but is soon led outside the knowable and predictable. She left these behind when she stepped out on this road. Both are in a process; we might analyse so from afar. But within there is no 'process'; instead lies a way through a wilderness, that might or might not be a road to somewhere. There are no certainties.

Whether driven by circumstance from what used to be, or led by some inner drawing, the wilderness tests the heart. The insulation of solid assumptions and the familiar routine have been removed, leaving exposed our deepest needs, emotions and desires. To add to this, the wilderness journey is made alone. I am not thinking of Jesus leaving behind the company of friends and family and going into a physical desert where no one made home. For the most part, in whatever wilderness we find ourselves there are other people around us; and often ones with whom we already have a relationship. And yet inwardly we feel ourselves alone. No one is able to make this journey for us; no one can be entirely with us, for all the desire they might have to do so. This is a deeply personal quest for meaning, for understanding, for resolution. Others can guide, support, suggest and encourage, and it is important to be open to receive whatever help is available for us. There will be ways in which one person's story mirrors another's and what has been learnt can be shared and found useful. Still, there is a place where no one else can enter, and no one else can choose or not choose to walk the uncertain road. This is also why we might find ourselves feeling distant from those we have been close to; how things were has gone and we do not yet know how things are to be, or even how *we* are to be. We do have ourselves for company, and how uncomfortable this is! The wilderness has a harsh and clear light that shows up every imperfection, and we have nowhere to go to escape our reality. There is less to engage the eye and the ear so we focus more intently on whatever is before us.

The breakdown of the expected has this way of facing us with ourselves. Imagine you are on your regular commute to work by train. There is trouble on the line; the train stops and time passes. Background details that on any other day would be insignificant begin to move into the foreground of your attention: the pattern of the seat fabric, the safety notices by the carriage door, the behaviour of the person sitting opposite you, the view from your window, the sound of an MP3 player somewhere further away. Our thoughts are loud too: 'When will we be on the move again? Why does this always seem to happen when I need to be somewhere? Why doesn't he turn down his music?' We go round in circles of thought and perception. Willing or not, we notice the seat fabric and every tear and blemish in it; we ask ourselves again: 'When will we be on the move?' Whatever wilderness we are travelling through – or feel completely lost and trapped in – we are brought into this sharpened, almost claustrophobic, attentiveness. We are confronted by the intensity of our sadness, our hunger to be loved or our insecurity. It is painful and raw to see so clearly. But such attentiveness also opens us to the presence of God.

The crystal fountain

Open now the crystal fountain,
whence the healing stream doth flow;
let the fire and cloudy pillar
lead me all my journey through.
Strong deliverer, strong deliverer,
be thou still my strength and shield;
be thou still my strength and shield.

There is no more immediate or driving need than thirst, and nothing so difficult to find in a desert than water. When the Israelites complain that for lack of anything to drink they will die, Moses takes a rod and strikes the great rock of Horeb, the mountain of God, and water flows.[5] In the Bible, it is thirst for water that represents the deepest of human longings, and a free-flowing stream God's gift of life. A Samaritan woman, unlucky in love and unhappy in life, meets Jesus at a well and is promised a spring of water welling up from within.[6] For Isaiah it is in the unlikely setting of the wasteland that hope is reborn and transformation begins. It is here that the blind will find sight and the tongue of the speechless will be set free to sing with joy, for 'waters shall break forth in the wilderness and streams in the desert'.[7] Nowhere more than in the wilderness do we become aware of our thirst – for meaning, for healing, for love, for belonging – and nowhere are we more open to receive what God continually desires to give: water that wells up from within, transforms, and brings forth life.

For the prophet Ezekiel, banished with his people to exile in Babylon, hope was hard to come by. Walking one day through a waterless valley his gaze fell on the dry bones scattered about him. Into his mind came the despairing cries of his neighbours and friends: 'Our bones are dried up, and our hope is lost; we are cut off completely.'[8] A valley is for water and water is for life but all he could see was the aridity of death. Then a question formed itself unexpectedly in his mind: 'Can these bones live?' He could not bring himself to find an answer. But into the silence came the word of the God he served: 'Come from the four winds, O breath, and breathe upon these slain that they may live . . . I will put my spirit within you, and you shall live, and I will place you in your own soil.'[9]

In leaving behind our former reality we also forgo any carefully deployed systems for keeping our deepest feelings and desires at bay. Our needs shout louder and will be heard. Like Ezekiel we have nowhere to go to escape the questions posed by the

---

5 Exodus 17.1–7
6 John 4
7 Isaiah 35.5–6
8 Ezekiel 37.11
9 Ezekiel 37.3, 9, 14

wilderness: 'Can these bones live? Can my life ever find a shape again? Will I ever belong?' We keep company with the wild beasts of our fears, hopes, loneliness, frustrations and longings. And yet this is also our passage into a greater depth of life, though it more often feels like our disintegration. The wild beasts are no more and no less than who we are; as we stay with them their cries grow less strangled and we learn their names. They have come not to destroy but to teach us. Within them lies the possibility of how life might be made anew. Breath shall pass through these dry bones and they shall live.

At the heart of Israel's religious and cultural life had been the Temple in Jerusalem, but now it lay in ruins, the symbolic expression of the crushing of a people's hope and expectation. Ezekiel, from a priestly family whose very identity revolved around Temple worship, must have felt devastated when he heard the news. Should this exile ever end there was nothing to return to. The past was gone; the house of God destroyed. And yet there stirred within Ezekiel the recognition of God's real and purposeful presence in this land of exile from home and hope. A vision passed through his mind of the Temple restored; and flowing from its threshold a mighty river, impossible to measure or to cross. As this river entered the stagnant, salt waters of the Arabah, its waters became fresh. Everything lived where the river flowed. Was it a dream, or a promise to build a future upon?[10]

For the Israelites in the wilderness, God provided a pillar of fire by night and a pillar of cloud by day to remind them of his presence. For Ezekiel, the vision of a mighty stream that made the bitter salt waters fresh. In the in-between time there are hints and glimpses to encourage us that this is after all a meaningful journey that will lead somewhere that corresponds with our deepest desires, even if nothing like any place we dared to imagine. Listen, look, pay attention and we understand, if only for a moment, that what is surfacing is not only a chaos capable of overwhelming us but a river of life. A day dawns when we feel an unfamiliar burst

---

10 Ezekiel 47.1–12

of energy; it may have neither rhyme nor reason that we can pin down but nevertheless it is there. It will not stay; the swirl of other feelings will remove it from our consciousness; but it is not entirely lost to us. Other moments come when we feel the pulse of this same elusive life-stream. There are moments of conversation when a pattern begins to suggest itself where there has only been muddle before. There is a glimmer of direction and purpose within our wandering. Perhaps we hear faint echoes of a voice: 'this is the way – walk in it.'[11] A random kindness provides encouragement for a moment when we feel low. There are other days when we have no such clarity. We sense we are simply and completely lost, and all suggestions that it might be otherwise no more than wishful thinking and illusion. The wilderness is a topsy-turvy place and rarely allows two days or two moments of consistent thinking. But then that energy again; that sense of being drawn by one who calls our name; that something that moves us to get up from the ground and start walking again that is more than wishful thinking: it is hope. The empty land is filled with presence. The vastness and void we have entered is also the height, length, breadth and depth of love beyond all knowing.

> I hear a voice I had not known.
> 'I relieved your shoulder from the burden
> Your hands were freed from the basket
> In distress you called, and I rescued you
> I answered you in the secret place of thunder.'[12]

The sound of silence

The wilderness is a place of encounter. Here Moses turned aside to see a bush burning but not consumed and heard God call his name. Ezekiel perceived the life-giving spirit of God breathing life into dead, dry bones. It is in the wilderness too that another

---

11 Isaiah 30.21
12 Psalm 81.5–7

prophet, Elijah, despairing of his life, gained a renewed sense of God with him and the courage to begin afresh. Ahab the King had vowed to kill him and Elijah was overcome with despondency. All that he had worked for seemed to have come to nothing:

> He went a day's journey into the wilderness, and came and sat down under a solitary broom tree. He asked that he might die: 'It is enough; now, O Lord, take away my life, for I am no better than my ancestors.'[13]

He sleeps, hoping for death, but an angel wakes him, telling him to 'get up and eat', and there before him is a cake baked on hot stones and a jar of water. Sleep comes again, and again the angel wakes him with food: 'Get up and eat, otherwise the journey will be too much for you.' For forty days and forty nights Elijah walks through the wilderness until he comes to 'Horeb, the mount of God.' There, where Moses turned aside to see a burning bush, Elijah becomes aware of the presence of God, not in earthquake, wind or fire but in 'the sound of sheer silence'. In the solitude of wilderness sheer silence sounds and a common bush burns. It is not that God dwells only in these wild places. Beneath the resident noise of every time and place, God 'is'; as Moses discovered, his name is I AM. But we are not always present to this presence; we ordinarily pass by the burning bush without a glance. At first all Elijah can hear is his own despair and Ahab's anger, and all he can see is his world overturned. But then he hears the silence that lies within, around, beyond and beneath the earthquake, wind and fire. He wraps his face in his cloak as one who stands before God.

One of the most effective ways I have found to help people begin to experience stillness is to ask them to close their eyes and give all their attention to listening. As thoughts arise – and they do – rather than seek to fight them off I suggest people allow them to come and go as if carried on a passing stream of water

---

13 This account of Elijah in the wilderness can be found in 1 Kings 19

and return to the physical act of giving all their attention to what they can hear. We hear the ticking clock, a car horn sounding somewhere outside, a shuffling of feet and rumbling of stomachs; and gradually, unexpectedly, the beginnings of silence. We think of silence as absence of noise; but everywhere there are sounds, sometimes physical, sometimes the emotional traffic of our different feelings. If silence were only to be found when feelings are wholly dormant and all external sounds removed, few of us would ever know it. But silence surrounds us and we can always step through its door; not despite our inward and outer noise but within it, and around it and beneath it. There are some words only spoken in silence. Moses hears his name called and Elijah understands he is not alone.

For the most part, the wilderness chooses us. Even when we take the initiative in setting a life change in motion we usually fail to anticipate how uncertain our existence will become and how much time and inner transformation must take place before we have any sense of arrival. Nevertheless we can willingly enter a wilderness place, recognizing that we stand in the need of the wisdom and clarity its starkness brings. There is no need to travel far; we can sit somewhere familiar and seek to be present as far as we can to who we are and who God is in this 'here' and this 'now'. Whereas at other times props will help us – reflections to consider, lines of thought to ponder and work through, a passage of scripture to read to stimulate our thinking – here we put these aside. It is enough to inwardly face God in faith that, as Moses discovered, the place where we are is holy ground.[14] Some of the speech in the silence will be our own: the expression of our true self, unmasked and free. Some will be of God. But we are unlikely to hear any words at all, for this conversation takes place in a deep and hidden place that former generations named our 'soul'. Relationship is being formed.

At other times we might decide to take a more extended time out, away from the familiar routine and the insistent call of the

14 Exodus 3.5

email or text message. More than ever before we are accessible to those who want to reach us, be they friends or foes. Presented as liberation and convenience, constant availability can easily become oppression. The line between work and play, the public arena and the private space is rubbed away. Because we can read the email from work – or because we are expected to – we are likely to do so. Everywhere we receive the gift of connectivity – or is it the imposition of control? In the early Christian centuries men and women went out from the city into the desert to escape the dulling of their spirit by the comforts and conventions of urban life. The need seems greater now. It is not peace we need but the disturbance that leads to peace. Whether we choose to go on a retreat offered by a religious house or to go on a walking pilgrimage, all that we leave behind brings us into confrontation with ourselves. The experience – at least at first – may be less warm glow than icy blast: the surfacing of buried questions and unwanted unease. The temptation is to escape back to the unreality that ordinarily drives us.

I woke up today troubled with unknown dreams. I am dissatisfied with a convenient life. I think of Abram who heard the Lord inviting him to set out across the wilderness for a land he did not know and I wonder if this is how he felt that challenge.[15] I imagine his thoughts: 'There is more to you, Abram, than the riches of land and property and a sure place in your self-made world.' But to set out and to leave all behind is fearful. I feel the draw to direct my life towards you, God, who summon me; but where will this lead me? And what about those easier ways I adopt to get by? So much less cost and so much less life. This is why you trouble me and I hear you in my dreams. You discomfort me.

The wilderness stretches between ending and beginning; between loss of meaning and its recovery; between awareness of deep longing and finding that which we long for; between questioning and the start of understanding; and it is a holy place of God's dwelling. Walking through the wilderness we enter into a

---

15 Genesis 12.1–3

new set of rules. We can stop and rest a while but this is no place to settle down or put down roots. We cannot grow crops or lay down sure supplies but each day there is unexpected daily bread. There will be water but not on tap. There will be no road map and the compass will often prove useless but now and then a pillar of fire will assure us that there is a way if only we consent to keep walking. We cannot make for ourselves a convenient god to do our bidding but a voice we do not know is all the while lifting the burden from our shoulders, helping us stand tall and strong as free people. We have exchanged easy answers for difficult questions, but the questions are closer to a truth that sets us free than the certainties we once built our life upon. We are growing into a dependency that unexpectedly liberates us. We do not have to know where we are going to; what matters is who is leading us there. We no longer have to be preoccupied with winning by sheer effort the daily bread of what we need because such bread is freely given. We grow more accustomed to this way of proceeding and receiving. Former comforts and securities are now revealed as burdens and encumbrances. The questions can narrow down to what really matters: 'How can I stay open to the one who leads me and provides for me?' Jesus says: 'I am the bread that gives life'; 'I am the way'.[16]

Maze or labyrinth?

I went with Nancy, seven years old, to Hampton Court Palace. One of the great attractions is the maze; certainly Nancy thought so. Free from my hand she ran into the maze with me in hot pursuit. We wandered round a while and then to my relief found our way out. Congratulating myself on my ability to work out the puzzle I relaxed too much and before I knew it Nancy had run in again. This time we got well and truly lost which Nancy found most amusing, careering here and there with me anxious to keep up in case we became separated. My frustration began to build as

---

16 John 6.35, 14.6

dead end followed dead end and promising paths proved be to no more than deceits. Fortunately we did find our way out; I am not writing this encompassed by hedges!

Some months later I walked a labyrinth. The experience was outwardly similar but in practice wholly different. In a labyrinth there is one path which, if followed, leads you to its centre and then back to where you first began. The labyrinth winds disconcertingly. At one moment the centre seems close, only for the path to loop away into obscurity. But there is no need to turn back; the path is purposeful; it leads unerringly to the centre. At times the sensation of being lost – of this all somehow being a trick – is still there; but there are no dead ends. The path knows where it is going even if you do not.

Is the way in the wilderness a maze or a labyrinth? Our sensations will suggest it is a maze, designed to confuse us and contain us in its grasp. But I understand it more as a labyrinth: a path that is in no measure direct and yet in its meandering *is* the way. The track followed is not inevitable; we do make choices that determine our direction. But what makes it more labyrinth than path is that God honours those choices we make and turns what might otherwise be dead ends into living beginnings. A pillar of fire by night, a pillar of cloud by day, God continues to guide, feed and provide, and to create a way through the wilderness where none seemed to be.

On the verge of Jordan

When I tread the verge of Jordan,
bid my anxious fears subside;
death of death and hell's destruction,
land me safe on Canaan's side.
Songs of praises, songs of praises,
I will ever give to thee;
I will ever give to thee.

The River Jordan stands as gateway to the Promised Land. For Williams it represents the transition from earthly to heavenly life;

death must be crossed as the Israelites crossed the stream that barred their path. The journey towards and through our death is the essence of the wilderness journey. Perhaps each wilderness journey we make through life prefigures this one defining movement into the unknown. In life we learn to die. If that sounds overly gloomy then let me put the other side: in dying we learn to live.

The wilderness awakes our fear yet helps us act fearlessly. We see how measured and safe we have been in our actions and how narrow our lives have thus become. The wilderness invites trust, and trust enables relationship, and this relationship gifts love which is life. Every act of trust is a kind of death, whereby we let go our anxious hold on life, and in so doing learn to live. This is not to say we make the passage easily. The verge of Jordan is trampled ground where many have paced up and down before making the crossing. Without the long schooling of the way in the wilderness we would not know how to face this moment. Thankfully there are songs to sing to awaken our courage: means whereby we can acknowledge our trepidation yet put our hope in a strong delivery intent on seeing us through to Canaan's side.

When in the wilderness

Williams' hymn and prayer *Guide me O thou great Jehovah*, suggests that all of life has the character of a wilderness walk. Whatever guidance we receive from God is partial: enough perhaps to suggest the next step but denying us the clarity of a well-formed path to a clear destination. We are more familiar with muddling through than marching ahead. The provision of God is real but rarely on our terms. A store of food within our control would be more comforting than the uncertainty of gazing into the sky wondering whether or not manna will fall today. God is present – sometimes even dramatically so – but also elusive, hiding in a cloud, refusing to appear or to act at the bidding of our will.

There are experiences that intensify this sense of vulnerable unknowing, and long stretches of time where we feel ourselves to be pilgrims lost in a barren land. But the truth is that our lives are always in process. The belief that we can be settled, sure and self-reliant for any length of time unravels in the face of ever-changing circumstance. Every relationship calls us forth, and bids us grow through our responding – the relationship with God more intensely than any other. God is not content to leave us in stable mediocrity. Amidst the shaking we are being formed, drawn out of the constrictions we have inhabited into the abundance of a land where milk and honey flow; but it rarely feels so!

Here are some suggestions for making the most of the way through the wilderness:

- *Keep walking*: Choose to trust that there is purpose and meaning to this journey even when you cannot see it.
- *Be open and aware*: This is a time of learning and discovery. The desert is a place of encounter. As you meet God whose name is I AM, you move into understanding of who YOU ARE.
- *Beware shortcuts*: We cannot go back to what was; it is no longer there. Nor can we ignore the call to make this journey without diminishing ourselves.
- *Accept dependence*: You do not know where you are going, but God does. You have no means of providing for yourself, but God gifts you daily bread.
- *Receive unexpected gifts*: In the wilderness a sudden shower of rain makes the barren land bloom. The hard and dry rock becomes the source of a spring of water.
- *Look for the pillar of fire*: Amidst the uncertainty you sense God's invitation to life or sense energy within that you cannot explain.
- *Hope in the Promised Land*: But don't become fixed in your ideas about where this land lies. Your life may take a different turn and lead you somewhere you could never have anticipated.

For reflection:

1] This chapter has centred on a hymn, *Guide me O thou great Jehovah.*

Read through its words slowly and reflectively. Stop if a phrase seems to speak to you. Ponder its significance for you. You might find this phrase has the quality of a prayer for you – one that you can hold before God.

Is there another hymn that sums up where you sense yourself to be today, or that puts into words what it is you are seeking or need? Again, reflect on its words and their significance for you at this time. Or sing it!

2] There has been a recent revival of interest in labyrinths. There is likely to be one in your local area. Set aside some time to walk it. Remember that the labyrinth is not a maze. A labyrinth has only one path; there are no blind alleys, though as you walk it you may feel that there are. Spend some time settling yourself down before you begin: perhaps just looking at the pattern, or stilling yourself before God. Walk the labyrinth path slowly, pausing when you want to. Let the path take you to the centre, where you may want to rest for a while. Then follow the same path out of the labyrinth. Relax into the experience; there is no need to force your thoughts in a particular direction. Let come what will come.

After a break it may be helpful to walk the labyrinth again. This time you are not so much looking for new insights as allowing a now more familiar path to lead you into a more receptive place within.

3] The Exodus journey through the wilderness was full of contradictions for those who took part in it:

- Anxiety about finding food and drink; the gift of manna from the skies, and water from the rock.

- The sensation of being lost and getting nowhere; the guiding presence of a pillar of fire by night and a pillar of cloud by day.
- Rebelling against God and succumbing to temptation; the formation of a covenant of trust and mutual commitment between the people and God.
- A time of everything familiar falling apart and breaking down; a time of being formed into a new creation.

How do these contradictions speak to your own wilderness experience? You may well find yourself in an in-between place, now feeling one thing and then the other.

4] This chapter has been about a journey through the unknown. Is there a character in a novel or film whose physical or interior journey you identify with in some way? What does their story say to yours?

7

Out of the Land of the Slave-Drivers

I have seen the miserable state of my people in Egypt; I have heard their appeal to be free of their slave-drivers. (Exodus 3.7)

For much of the time I have suggested that we own struggle and difficulty as a natural part of our human experience. There are indeed growing pains, and no life is free from loss and the sadness and bewilderment it can bring. The focus of a fully human life is not the avoidance of pain but the generous expression of who we are in a way that is life-giving for those around us; even if this might hurt now and then. But not all suffering flows from such positive intent; sometimes we are ensnared in patterns of thought and action that diminish us and prevent our growth. More often than not they also have some harmful impact on others. At the simplest level most of us will have fallen into a sulk now and then. We don't want to accept reality because it isn't what we planned or wanted. For as long as the mood lasts we cannot move on and others cannot engage with us. Most of us are not so consistently mature that we don't sometimes hold on to 'the injustice of it all' longer than is helpful to ourselves or others. But what if our thoughts become set in self-destructive patterns that become so familiar that it proves difficult to recognize the harm they do or to escape them? A sulk will pass, but what if I consistently believe that all are against me, or that everything I do is doomed to fail? Who or what will set me free if I inwardly reject and fear who I am? Our thoughts can provide a more effective prison than walls of stone and iron bars. Like the slave-drivers of Israel in Egypt, they burden and oppress us, locking us into misery.

In George Eliot's novel *Silas Marner*[1] a weaver is unjustly accused of a crime by members of his church. Hurt beyond measure, he rejects God, the community of those he once considered friends and the possibility of new relationships. He moves to a new area, gives himself to his weaving, and finds some solace in counting the money he earns but has no use for. Silas shrinks down his life until it is manageable and inviolable. If no one gets near to him then no one will hurt him. He builds walls to keep others out; but they also shut him in. Year follows year, marked only by the monotonous rhythm of his loom and the increase of his money. Until the day comes when his gold is stolen and his defences are ruptured:

> To any one who had observed him before he lost his gold, it might have seemed that so withered and shrunken a life as his could hardly be susceptible of a bruise . . . But in reality it had been an eager life, filled with immediate purpose, which fenced him in from the wide, cheerless unknown. It had been a clinging life; and though the object round which its fibres had clung was a dead disrupted thing, it satisfied the need for clinging. But now the fence was broken down – the support was snatched away.

A 'withered and shrunken' life; a life 'fenced in' and 'clinging'; a life centred on 'a dead and disrupted thing'. Silas is a victim of injustice, but also of his own fear. It is not just outward circumstances, however difficult they might be, that act as the slave-driver and gaoler; it is the inner landscape of our beliefs and attitudes.

Desolation or consolation?

Ignatius Loyola, the founder of the Jesuits and author of *The Spiritual Exercises,* had a particular term for the condition whereby

---

1 George Eliot, *Silas Marner: A Weaver of Raveloe*, first published in 1861.

people are caught in ways of thinking that are life-denying and destructive: *desolation*. His use of the word is not identical to ours. Desolation for Ignatius is not the grief of bereavement; nor is it simply an alternative word for unhappiness. Nor is desolation in this sense a medical condition, such as clinical depression. To begin to get inside Ignatius' use of the term we need to understand certain basic assumptions he makes about God, humanity and the meaning of our existence. He sums these up at the beginning of the *Exercises* in what he terms 'the first principle and foundation':

Humankind is created for a relationship of love with God, for by this means we are made whole.

Everything that exists has the potential to help us move towards this end, for all comes from God and is good.

However what matters is attaining a life of love in God, not the possession of things. Where the gifts of creation help us attain our goal we are to use them, but when they become an obstacle, we are to let them go.

Therefore we are not to be bound by our needs and desires. We should not be so attached to health, riches, the good opinion of others, or our safety that we become unable to respond freely to God's invitation; for illness, the lack of possessions, the loss of our good name, or exposure to risk can also be means by which we are led more deeply into life.

Our guiding principle in all the choices we make is to discern what better serves to lead us to our goal: our wholeness and freedom through the growth of God's life in us.[2]

---

2 This is my own interpretation of Ignatius' 'Principle and Foundation'. I have sought to be true to its spirit rather than provide a word-by-word translation.

Ignatius' concern is with what he sees as the origin and natural direction of human life. God is the source and centre of our being. If we assent to this truth in action then his life grows in us, and our lives rest in their natural place of balance. We develop into the fullness of who we are by being in relationship with God, who in love goes on creating us. This is to be our choice, over and above anything else, for in taking any other path we are moving against who we are at depth. Throughout the *Spiritual Exercises*, Ignatius understands that the Holy Spirit is the experience of God within, summoning us into relationship with God through Christ and therefore into life. This life has a particular quality that Ignatius sums up in the traditional terms of faith, hope and love. Faith is the capacity to live in trust. The root of this trust is the recognition that all comes as gift of a generous God. Therefore we do not need to fear, nor grab what we need beyond what God provides. Hope is not, as we sometimes use the word, wishful thinking. Wishful thinking seeks to escape the reality of the here and now and move to a fantasy land. Hope always begins with how things are; it is founded on realism. However hope knows that because God is ever-present and wholly committed to his creation there is endless possibility. Love is the large-heartedness of God, that always has room for the other, and ever seeks to give itself for the others' sake. The source of such a life is the Holy Spirit or, in Ignatius' own words, the 'good spirit'.[3] When one is moved by the Spirit then one lives in faith, hope and love as God desires, and Ignatius calls this 'consolation'.[4]

In contrast, desolation is a state of being whose source is not the Spirit but what Ignatius describes as 'the enemy of our human nature'[5] – in other words, all that works against the beauty and

---

3 Quotations from the Spiritual Exercises are taken from: Louis J. Puhl S.J., 1951, *The Spiritual Exercises of St. Ignatius: Based on studies in the language of the autograph*, Chicago: Loyola University Press. For Ignatius' use of the term 'good spirit' see examples in his 'rules for discernment of spirits', sections 314 & 315.

4 Section 316

5 Section 327

giftedness of our creation in God. When the source of our thoughts is 'the enemy of our human nature' we are inclined not to faith but instead to anxiety, not to hope but rather to despair, and not to love but to self-absorption. We are moving not towards relationship founded on love but isolation driven by fear.

Consolation and desolation are therefore related to the *source* of our attitudes and the *direction* they take us in. Consolation flows from and to God and leads us into a fully human life. Desolation stems from what is opposed to the movement of God in our lives and drives us to live in a way that diminishes our potential and that is harmful to others. A person can be in deep pain through bereavement, or thrown about by the turmoil of events and yet be in consolation, if in that struggle she rests her life more deeply in God. The trouble she experiences can yet become life-giving. On the other hand someone can be outwardly content through getting their own way and having life in their control and yet be in desolation. Silas Marner's existence up the point his gold is taken is coherent in its own terms but it hardly deserves the term 'life'; he is dead to the world around him, and dead to so much in himself.

The enemy of our human nature

So what or who is 'the enemy of our human nature' that Ignatius identifies as the source of our desolation? Ignatius also refers to 'the evil one', 'Satan' or the 'evil spirit'.[6] It might be that we begin to picture a devil figure, perhaps complete with horns and forked tail, and at this point we either switch off because it seems so unbelievable or begin to worry that we are in some way possessed. Neither approach seems helpful to me. On the one hand experience tells us that we can be in the grip of attitudes that have a destructive quality about them; we ignore this reality at the peril of our own wellbeing. On the other, we are not inherently evil or

---

6 Sections 329, 142, 315

in the power of an independent, malevolent being equivalent to God – a Destroyer to balance the Creator.

My sense of what Ignatius means by desolation is the playing out of what is hurt and damaged within us in our attitudes and actions. It flows from 'the enemy of our human nature' in the sense that these responses move against the truth of who we are in God. Desolation stems from the cumulative wear and tear of humankind's capacity to be destructive. Because of our experience, or through what we have been taught or have observed in others, the life of faith, hope and love may seem alien or unattainable. It feels safer to turn inwards and defend ourselves, rather than trust in another's goodness. Many of us have little faith in ourselves. Perhaps we breathed in an unintended put-down, or interpreted another's inability to respond to our need as evidence of our unfitness for love. Or perhaps an over-anxious parent passed on a fear of life itself. It might have been that as a child we worked out that the way to survive was to fit in with the expectations of others and squash down anything that worked against this. Alternatively we may have found our security in being the dominant force, making sure things happened the way we wanted them in so far as we had power to do so; and sometimes at others' expense. Or maybe in the absence of love we could feel sure about, we found comfort in the possession of objects or in actions that, at least for a while, blunted our loneliness. After a while these ways of thinking and being become less about active choice and more about habit – our place of habitation. This is the story of all of us, though with infinite variation of degree and emphasis. It becomes an effort to step out of these houses – they are 'home' after all, however uncomfortable and cramped they might turn out to be.

The awakening

'Evil' is 'live' spelt backwards; we are facing and moving in the wrong direction: in opposition to what is God-given, relational and creative. It hurts us. It goes against the grain of our human nature. Desolation is difficult to escape, but is also draining to maintain. Clench your fists tightly and after a while you will want to open them up and allow your hands to relax. Before the loss of his gold, Silas Marner lives a clenched-fist life: tightly bound, closed to meaningful contact, continually on the defensive. He is afraid of what might happen if he opens his hands. But the fear is eroding his life away: he is physically worn and his spirit is dim. However, a residual spark of life will not allow him to dwindle into nothingness. The circumstance is brutal: the casual act of a thief robs him in a moment of all he has worked for through long and lonely years. His treasured gold is gone. It is as if his fingers have been prised open by force and now he has nothing to shelter him – but also nothing to prevent him receiving an invitation into life. One day an orphaned little girl wanders into his house. Silas recognizes one lost like himself and sees in the child's golden hair his lost treasure returning back to him. When questions arise as to what is to happen to the child, Silas is moved to say he will care for her. Gradually the girl he names Eppie leads him out of the cramped and lonely existence he has woven for himself:

> Unlike the gold which needed nothing, and must be worshipped in close locked solitude – which was hidden away from the daylight and deaf to the song of the birds – Eppie was a creature of endless claims and ever-growing desires, seeking and loving sunshine, and living sounds, and living movements; making trial of everything, with trust in new joy, and stirring the human kindness in all eyes that looked on her . . . The gold had asked that he should sit weaving longer and longer, deafened and blinded more and more to all things except the monotony of his loom and the repetition of his web; but Eppie called him away from his weaving, and made him think all its pauses a holiday, reawakening his senses with her fresh life.

Silas the weaver can neither hear nor see until the child draws him back into life. The world of repetitive loom and absence of relationship was in part the fruit of the injustice Silas suffered, but was also the result of how he chose to respond to it. Maybe the strands of trust and openness were never well formed in him, and it did not take too much to tip him over into despair. The child's coming was pure gift; but it was also down to Silas to sense the invitation of the moment. He allowed himself to be moved and to step out of his isolation. I see echoes of Silas' reawakening in the New Testament account of the raising of Lazarus from death. Jesus tells his friend to come forth from the tomb. He bids those around the now living man to 'unbind him and let him go.'[7] Whatever we make of the story, for me it stands as symbol of Christ's call to step out of the lifelessness of self-made prisons into the freedom and expansiveness of faith, hope and love. Silas, like Lazarus, is called out of the tomb. He is unbound and set free. And it is his response to the vulnerability of a lost child that works this miracle in his life.

Driven or free?

Desolation or consolation; the worship of gold or the risk of caring for the child Eppie; Lazarus bound in the tomb or Lazarus walking free: are we being moved by the Spirit or being driven against our God-given nature? Ignatius is clear that consolation is a gift of God rather than something we manufacture, and that desolation is not always a state of being that we will or cling to. Yet, as with Silas, our choices do have significance. What way do we want our life to face? Which inner voice will we listen to? Ignatius focuses the question in his meditation on the 'Two Standards'.[8]

One standard belongs to Christ 'our supreme leader and lord' and the other to 'Lucifer, the deadly enemy of our human nature'.[9] The language uncomfortably plunges us into the imagery and language of sixteenth-century Spain, with its militaristic air and the personification of the 'enemy of our human nature' in Lucifer, the fallen angel. Being asked to consider whose flag we

---

7 John 11.44
8 Sections 136–48
9 Section 136

wish to stand beneath may seem neither helpful nor relevant. Yet a careful examination of the tone of the conflicting calls reveals a radical difference in their characters. Whilst the enemy 'goads', and 'binds with chains', tempting us to 'covet riches . . . and the empty honours of this world',[10] Christ stands 'in a lowly place', his appearance 'beautiful and attractive'.[11] Christ recommends 'his servants and friends to seek to help all . . . by attracting them to the highest spiritual poverty.'[12] The enemy *forces*, *compels*, *drives* . . . Christ *attracts*, *calls*, *recommends*. If we are acting compulsively, driven by some need or fear, then what moves us is not of God. Invitation and free response is the mark of Christ's call to relationship. The difference can be subtle. At times we need the push of a sense of obligation or an externally imposed guideline to do the generous and needful thing. But if the whole of our existence echoes with 'oughts', 'shoulds' and 'musts' then we are driven, not free. Perhaps a need to have others think well of us has become our slave-driver.

Christ *invites*, and what is destructive and self-diminishing *drives*. In the Gospel of John Jesus contrasts the motives and actions of a shepherd and a thief towards a flock of sheep.[13] The shepherd is willing, if it comes to it, to lay down his life for his sheep. The sheep choose to follow him, hearing the sound of his voice calling them each by name. They go in and go out freely and find pasture. On the other hand the thief sneaks in to the sheepfold by stealth, determined to take the sheep away by force. Jesus as shepherd has come 'so that they may have life and have it to the full.' In contrast the focus of the thief is 'to steal, kill and destroy'. The relationship with Christ is described as one of freedom and friendship, characterized by choice, not compulsion. Ignatius believes we can only truly learn and live in this freedom through centring in all things on God, who loves us without condition. If we make anything else our centre – for example, the love

---

10 Section 142
11 Section 144
12 Section 146
13 John 10:1–11

of riches, honour, or comfort – it will betray us, bind us, goad and confine us. We will live more in the narrow fear of losing what we have, than in the spaciousness of love.

It matters then, to be able to tell the difference between these two inward movements: one that ultimately diminishes our being and one that sets the true self free. Discernment is the keystone of Ignatius' thought. If we are to choose what keeps us in life-giving relationship with God, and turn from what takes us from this centre, then we need to become more deeply aware of the patterns of thinking and feeling that ordinarily drive our actions and responses. We must also be able to gain a deeper sense of what the 'voice' or 'touch' of the Spirit sounds/feels like, and distinguish this from other, more destructive impulses. Ignatius is keenly aware what a muddle the inner world of our thoughts and feelings can be, and how difficult this work of discernment is. He therefore supplies those involved in guiding others through the *Exercises* some guidelines for distinguishing the movement of the 'good spirit' from that of the 'enemy of our human nature'. Though these guidelines belong to that setting, there are principles within them that may be useful more generally.

Where are you going?

The invitation issued by Jesus is 'follow me'.[14] To respond is to set out on a path; to deliberately choose a direction. This road, as Ignatius understands it, takes us into, rather than away from, our human nature. It helps us 'be' in a way that is self-expressive, liberated and fruitful because we are walking deeper into the land of faith, hope and love. It opens us to the working of God who continues to call our true self forth and to heal us of our hurts and fears. Ignatius suggests that we experience this summons to life in different ways depending on our established life-orientation:

---

14 Mark 1.17

When the disposition is contrary to those of the spirits they enter with noise and commotion that are easily perceived. When the disposition is similar to that of the spirits, they enter silently, as one coming into his own house when the doors are open.[15]

If we are on a self-destructive path the voice of the Spirit may come with a sharp sting; something jolts us and makes us recognize we are on a road to nowhere. The voice of the 'enemy of our human nature', however, may encourage us to meet our immediate needs and not listen to the signs within that warn us we are going down a dead end. As a young person I went through a period of under-eating. I hesitate to call it anorexia – I wasn't even aware of the existence of such a condition – but it had something of that character. Life felt difficult and beyond what I was up to and the one thing that I had control of was how much I did or did not eat. Not eating more than I allotted myself proved a strange and seductive comfort. I had bouts of most miserable illness but continued on my path. But one day a sharp voice surfaced in my conscious-ness: 'What you are doing to yourself is stupid.' It wasn't quite as dramatic as Saul cast to the ground by blinding light on the road to Damascus yet it had something of that stinging quality – and I listened.

If, on the other hand, we are seeking God and wanting to move towards fullness of life for ourselves and others then Ignatius suggests the work of the Spirit will be marked by an inner attraction and by joy, energy and peace. This 'consolation' is manifest in 'every increase in hope, faith and love, and all interior joy that invites and attracts to what is heavenly and to the salvation of one's soul by filling it with peace and quiet in its Creator and Lord.'[16] On the other hand, the work of the 'enemy' – those destructive, life-denying tendencies we have learnt to inhabit – will be to 'harass with anxiety, afflict with sadness' and to 'raise

---

15 Section 335
16 Section 336

obstacles backed by fallacious reasonings.'[17] My guess is that you will recognize this pattern. Someone decides that he will say what he really thinks rather than keep a false and uncomfortable silence. But then self doubt seeps in: 'Am I doing the right thing? What if it all goes horribly wrong? Maybe it's better to leave it this time.' What follows is often self-recrimination, and a sense that nothing will ever change; it is hopeless to even try. Ignatius describes this 'desolation' as 'darkness of soul, turmoil of spirit' that results in 'want of faith, want of hope, want of love.' Our spirit becomes 'wholly slothful, tepid, sad and separated . . . from its Creator and Lord.'[18]

Think about where a course of action leads you

We must carefully observe the whole course of our thoughts. If the beginning and middle and end of the course of our thoughts are wholly good and directed towards what is entirely right, it is a sign that they are from the good angel. But the course of thoughts suggested to us may terminate in something evil, or distracting, or less good than the soul had originally proposed to do. Again it may end in what weakens the soul, or disquiets it; or by destroying the peace, tranquillity, and quiet which it had before, it may cause disturbance to the soul. These things are a clear sign that the thoughts are proceeding from the evil spirit, the enemy of our progress and eternal salvation.[19]

Jesus said 'the tree is known by its fruit.'[20] Sometimes a course of action seems, on the surface, attractive, but when we reflect on it we see that it draws us into a place of fear. It closes in our world rather than opening out the possibility of growth. On the other hand, a course of action may look difficult, but following it leads

---

17 Section 315
18 Section 317
19 Section 333
20 Matthew 12.33

us into greater faith in God; to life opening up rather than closing in; and to a deeper respect for ourselves and others. Because we tend to revisit the same situation more than once, it can help to look back and see the fruit of the choices we consciously or unconsciously made. We might ask ourselves: 'Did this choice produce the benefit I expected? Might the alternative path I rejected so quickly have been more life-giving in the longer run? What fear or need seems to drive me?' On the other hand, if we are seeking the good and the true, the work of Spirit of God has a sense of invitation: an unfamiliar quickening of our own spirit. We look back and see that however challenging this stepping out of our pattern was, we felt energy and purposefulness when we saw it through.

Gradually we become familiar with the tone of the Spirit's invitation and more skilled in distinguishing this from other, louder voices. Imagine going to meet a friend in a packed country pub. The noise is such that it seems impossible to conduct a conversation. But a strange thing happens: we gradually tune in to the one voice we want to attend to and tune out those that are unnecessary until we can hear quite clearly. The cacophony of sounds remains but now only as background. It works so well. But then a person near us says something interesting, and before we know it we have lost our focus and can't hear any more. We turn ourselves deliberately to be attentive again and the conversation resumes. Amidst the chorus of sounds running through our muddled lives is the call of one who invites us into life. Hitherto we might have only heard the loud, insistent voices of those who knowingly or unknowingly diminished us or led us into fear; but now we hear this invitation, not so much outside us as within our own spirit. The fears and compulsions may still be insistent and may in the end have their way; but we have heard this other voice, and if we continue and do not despair of ourselves or of God, we shall hear it again. It is as if we have lived our lives in a small narrow room and now someone has opened a door and we see there is, after all, another and larger space that we can step into. I am not, as I once thought, a 'hopeless case', incapable of change. Another is within me and enabling me to go where I hitherto feared to.

It is a voice of faith; not just in this other who invites me but also in myself. It is a voice of love: a drawing me forth that is kindly and compassionate, taking me out of loneliness and into relationship.

Knowing our vulnerability

We are vulnerable in different places, perhaps to do with our story or the echoing voice of someone in our past who taught us to fear or to disown who we are. Knowing where and how a destructive flow of thought or responding enters is not in itself the solution to our difficulty, but it can be the beginning of not being swept away by its force.

We had been having trouble with the roof for a while. When the rain was heavy and the wind in a particular direction we would hear the tell-tale dripping of water in the passageway outside our bedroom. Going into the loft I could see the trail of dampness on the rafters; but where was the water coming from? There was no obvious hole. Various attempts to seal this or that area of roof hadn't worked out. Where the water appeared was not necessarily where the water was getting in. Water has a way of finding the one weak point in the structure and then seeping through tiles and roof felt until it finds a convenient place to fall. The crucial task went beyond simply noting where the water was falling: what was its trail, and where did it make its entry in the first place?

I remember a morning when I felt positive, hopeful and energized about the future. The anxiety and self-absorption that had long dogged my progress seemed to be ebbing away and self-belief was growing in its place. And then I went for a walk in the country. The scenery was wild and beautiful – everything that feeds my spirit. But in the corner of a field someone had carelessly dumped their rubbish. As the day wore on my mood changed. I began to feel restless and aware of my tiredness. I judged that someone has been less than sensitive to me. Doubt weaved its way through the hope I had previously enjoyed. By the end of the day I felt completely hopeless, cut off from those around me, sullen and resentful. When I revisited what had happened to me, I realized that the turning point had been the sight of that rubbish in the field. Though I had few thoughts about it at the time – beyond anger that someone could have been so thoughtless – it was as if at that moment someone had said to me, 'Who are you to think you can make something of yourself when there's so much unresolved rubbish in your life?' That was where the water got in – the moment when the spiralling down into unhappy self-absorption began. What the rubbish in the field said was not true but it was powerful in its untruth. It took me into thoughts more familiar than the faith and hope I had been held in for a brief while.

Ignatius suggests that when we so recognize our desolation we make our anchor point what we saw when in consolation. What was I feeling before I saw the rubbish in the field? What path had I set myself on? How did I then sense God's invitation? It can also help to seek out the wise counsel of one whose judgement we trust. Ignatius suggests that at times the enemy of our human nature acts as a secret agent, subtly undermining our progress towards wholeness.[21] If we keep our struggling to ourselves, whether through shame or fear of rejection, we may become prey to paralysing self-accusatory thoughts. Often we only begin to accept ourselves through the acceptance of another. Through sharing we move into a healthier and truer perspective: 'Yes, there is rubbish in the field, but the field is good, and God is working with me to clear it away.'

Acting into a new way of thinking

It helps to positively move against the flow of thoughts and attitudes arising during a time of desolation. This signals our intent not to go down the same old road. Our turning in the direction we want to go enables God to begin to make this movement possible. Having said this, I am not sure how fruitful it is to attempt

---

21 See section 334

to think ourselves into a new way of acting. For many years I have worked with volunteers in the field of social care. More than once I have seen how someone shows enormous generosity in meeting the needs of vulnerable people in the community yet neglects to look after her own basic human needs. She finds it hard – almost impossible – to say 'no'. She gives herself no proper time of rest or recreation. What she snatches for her own needs are the poor scraps of time and attention left over when everyone else's needs are catered for. It might look like the height of Christian generosity – the Gospel lived out fully. But there is a hole: she doesn't feel herself to be worthy of a tenth of the care she extends to others. Eventually she is likely to burn out, there being nothing to sustain her own inner life. How is she to move towards loving herself in the same way as her neighbour? She can stand in front of a mirror each day and repeat to herself, 'I am worthy of love and care.' It might help. But I suspect it would be more useful to attempt to act herself into a new way of thinking. She might decide to keep one day each week entirely free for herself, or to spend some money on a holiday, or to take time out regularly to go swimming, an activity she remembers she enjoyed in the past. When we cannot seem to think ourselves into a new way of acting it may be profitable to act ourselves into a new way of thinking.

It needs to be said again: desolation is no simple equivalent to unhappiness, even though the two are often intertwined. It is not unhealthy to experience a deep sense of sadness, or to feel the pain of being alone when what we long for is the company of one we love. If we seek at all costs to avoid or remove the struggle and sorrow that living and loving involve then we also deny their gift. The Jesus of the Gospels is a fully alive and sometimes hurting human being. The abundant life he lives and invites us into is not devoid of difficulty, struggle and sorrow. Avoidance of reality is a form of desolation. Jesus' ministry begins with a testing in the wilderness, when the path of desolation surfaces attractively in his consciousness: 'make yourself comfortable outside of God's provision . . . put your God to the test to see if he really cares for you . . . use your power to have dominion over others and make them serve your need.'[22] Later, when on the road to Jerusalem and to the confrontation that he recognized would likely lead to his death, he fiercely rounded on Peter's suggestion that he save himself.[23] My sense is that he was not so much criticizing Peter as turning against his own inclination to lead life fearfully and outside trust. As the moment passes Jesus goes on to explain: 'For those who want to save their life will lose it . . . for what will it profit them if they gain the whole world but forfeit their life?'[24] The ruination of the life of faith, hope and love is the deeper unhappiness.

Tools for listening

Ignatius wrote *The Spiritual Exercises* as a handbook for guides supporting people who were seeking a deeper openness to God in all things. He recognized from the ups and downs of his own experience how difficult it can be to discern the invitation of Christ amidst the crowded room of our memories, feelings, thoughts and desires. For most of us there will be a great deal to unlearn and to disentangle. It will take time and practice to sense which instincts and desires we can trust and which to be wary of. Is it for that reason he makes this an accompanied journey. Those who work alongside others in this way are sometimes called 'spiritual directors'. The term is unhelpful if we understand it as a dependency on someone who is going to tell us what to do. The guide's role is to help discern with the one he accompanies the direction of the Spirit. He encourages his 'directee' to go with this flow. John of the Cross, himself a spiritual guide for many, put it this way:

> Those who guide people should realise that the principal agent and guide and motive force in this matter is not them, but the

---

22 This is my summary of the temptations Jesus experiences in the wilderness, as told in Luke 4.1–13.

23 Matthew 16.21–3

24 Matthew 16.25–6

Holy Spirit, who never fails to care for his people. They are only instruments to guide people to perfection by faith and the law of God, according to the Spirit that God is giving to the individual person . . . so his whole concern should be to see whether he can recognise where God is carrying them and if he cannot, leave them alone and do not disturb them.[25]

Beyond the experience of a retreat such as the *Exercises*, it can help to have such a reference point for the journey into life through relationship with God. It is not easy to work our way through the self-diminishing attitudes we have breathed in through our past, or to trust the invitation to life we so tentatively hear in the present. There are many who are trained and skilled in this ministry and offer it generously to those seeking it.

A second tool is what is referred to in the *Exercises* as the *Examen*, sometimes called the examination of conscience or examination of consciousness. This is the regular practice of reflecting back on our experience. Each day – even one that seems quite uneventful – is rich in content. Different things happen; a variety of thoughts and emotions pass through us or stubbornly stick around. There are unexpected gifts; often missed unless deliberately recalled. We see something that gladdens our heart for a moment before the pace of the day sweeps it away. Yet it is not lost; rather it waits for us to summon it back into our memory. Somewhere in all the mix we might have sensed an invitation from God; not pressed into our consciousness with the clarity of a signed note, but there all the same if we only stop to consider. We might also have met our unbelieving self, choosing or being driven unwillingly along a path of desolation. Ignatius suggests we spend some time each day listening to our lives, our thoughts and our feelings, and that we do so in the company of God. We

---

25 Kieran Kavanaugh and Otilio Rodriguez, 1979, 'The Living Flame of Love', stanza 3.46 from *The Collected Works of St. John of the Cross*, translated by Kieran Kavanaugh and Otilio Rodriguez, Washington: ICS Publications.

approach this time asking God to help us see, hear and under-stand. It is this daily practice that helps us meet God in the ordinary, and to recognize and turn from what has oppressed us in the past.

A third tool is the keeping of a journal. This goes hand in hand with the *Examen*. Recording reflections upon experience on a regular basis can reveal patterns and movement. The same questions come up; is it time to give them more serious attention? We become aware that what seems like a disconnected series of events and responses in fact has a pattern; a clear sense of direction is emerging.

Do we ever come to a point when our capacity to be sunk into desolation is no more? I don't think so; at least it hasn't happened to me yet. Perhaps what does happen is that we become more attuned to when we are moving in a self-destructive direction. We more readily recognize our points of vulnerability and get more practised at side-stepping them. But we still have our bad days, and they serve as reminders of our need of God. Wherever we are and however we are, God is compassionately and generously alongside us. I think of the 23rd Psalm in this way. Even when we walk in the dark valleys of our desolation, God is there. In the presence of our foes, including those that stem from our own vulnerability, God provides for us. And those tantalizing final lines: 'I shall dwell in the house of the Lord my whole life long.' I once saw this as a reference to heaven; an eternal dwelling place won through to at the end of much struggling. But it is here and now that the invitation comes to make our home in the Lord. With faith and with hope we step out of our fears, over the threshold into the house of Love.

For prayer and reflection

1] God in my Day

This is an awareness exercise to be used on a daily basis as a way of becoming more aware of where we meet God within outward events and our inner thoughts and feelings. It will probably take five to ten minutes. It can also be a prayerful way of letting our day go into God's hands so that we don't carry our anxieties and frustrations unobserved and unhealed into our sleep and into a new day.

1. Events of today

Like watching a video, I replay the day, letting God prompt my memory, and remind me of significant things that happened in my day, or insights that I gained.

2. Thanksgiving

I thank God for the gifts of the day that have gone: the kindnesses shown me; the things that lifted my spirits – no matter how small.

3. Feelings experienced

I become aware of what I felt today and ask God to show me why I felt as I did.

4. Your call to me

I ask God to show me in what ways he asked something of me today . . .

- in my dealings with people
- in the way I treated myself
- in anything I previously sensed I was called to do.

I review how I responded.

5. Forgiveness and healing

I bring to God anything that I need forgiveness for, trusting in God's readiness to forgive.

I bring to God anything from my day I need healing for, trusting in God's love that casts out fear, and binds up wounds.

6. Trust in God for the day to come

I let go to God any anxieties I have about the day to come.

I ask God for the gift of what I most need for the day ahead.

2] Clenched fist and open hand

Clench your fists so that your fingers dig deeply into the palm of the hand. Feel the tension and constriction. Look at your fingers tightly bound, the blood flow constricted in your knuckles. Here is your anxiety about the future, your ill-ease and discomfort; your holding fast of what does not satisfy; your fear of being who you are.

God comes to you with open hands: tender and compassionate hands; generous, welcoming hands; waiting, inviting hands.

Now slowly release the tension in your fingers; watch as they slowly unfurl. Let your fingers stretch and play, your palms open and relaxed before you. You are ready now to let go; ready now to receive; ready now to express who you are.

Repeat the action: now clenching your fists, now letting your hands relax and open.

God of the open hands,
I give you my clenched fists.
Release me from the grip of fear,
that I may receive all you desire to share.

8

Meeting and Separation

There are two forms of friendship; meeting and separation . . . when two beings who are not friends are near each other there is no meeting and when friends are far apart there is no separation. As both forms contain the same good thing, they are both equally good. (Simone Weil)[1]

They have taken away my Lord

Simone Weil cuts across what appears to be a natural and clear division: separation happens in the absence of meeting and meeting brings separation to an end. Friends, she suggests, can be far apart and yet together. The pain of missing one you love and the joy of being united again are two very different expressions of the presence of relationship. The experience of the relationship changes, but not its reality.

One of the most poignant of the stories in the Gospels sees Mary Magdalene searching for the body of Jesus. It is early morning, and still dark. She has slept little. When she finds the tomb empty she feels a double pain: Jesus had been taken away from her in life, now he has been removed from her in death. Mary stands there weeping, repeating the same sentence to those who question her: 'They have taken away my Lord and I do not know where they have laid him.'[2] Loss is surely the deepest of wounds.

---

1 Simone Weil, 2009, *Waiting for God*, New York: First Harper Perennial Modern Classics Edition, p. 84

2 John 20.13

Grief can overwhelm us, leading us into what feels like a kind of madness where all we have thought of as normal is overthrown. Yet the very intensity of the experience of separation tells us of the intimacy of the meeting that has taken place. We miss those we most love, whether they are divided from us by death or distance or circumstance, and in our loss we are still united with them.

Meeting and separation, and the pleasure and pain they bring, are also characteristic of our encounter with God. The insistent message of the Scriptures is that God desires to be one with us, and yet when we seek God what we sometimes experience is his elusiveness; or even more than this, his absence. There are times of meeting. Some of these are experiences that so mark us that we sense life can never be the same. Others are quieter, more every-day moments of awareness. But there are also troubling times of separation, and not always because we are the ones who have wandered away. The closer the contact has been the more this absence is felt, and the deeper the longing for what has been lost.

Psalm 42 is imprinted on my memory. This is not so surprising given that for three years I sung it every Sunday in church. It was the one psalm we had a tune to and the guitarist knew how to play. The psalm is the song of one who feels wrenched apart from his homeland and the God who has guarded his life thus far. Line by line it twists and turns in puzzlement and hurt. How can the one who has become 'my help and my God', 'the God of my life', 'my rock', now leave him to himself. 'Why have you forgotten me?' he cries. When someone who means a great deal to us is with us, we might in some way take them for granted. It is when they are gone that we see more intensely how intertwined our two lives have become. Had they been nothing to us their leaving would not wound us so deeply. Then, like this exile, we yearn for what we have lost:

As a deer longs for flowing streams
So my soul longs for you my God.[3]

---

3 Psalm 42.1

Why then, if God desires relationship with us, and we for our part are drawn into seeking him, do we experience absence alongside presence? Why this thirsting for lost, flowing streams? Why is Mary left at the empty tomb, desolate and weeping?

Someone is missing

To begin our exploration we need to go back, and further than we might think. When does relationship begin? The sensible answer would seem to be when two beings first consciously encounter one another. However, Christian tradition suggests that in our meeting with God the roots of the relationship exist from the very beginning. On the one hand this is because we are inwardly shaped for intimacy with God and thus find ourselves drawn into longing for what we lack. On the other, because there has never been a moment when God has not sought us.

There is unease at work in most of us that might be summed up in the words of the U2 song: 'I still haven't found what I'm looking for.' I know my own incompleteness even though I am generously blessed in the people I know, the beauty I see and the everyday experiences that delight me. There are quiet moments when I meet this restlessness in me. I can put different names to it: 'I am struggling to be free'; 'I still don't know who I am'; 'I want to be comfortable in my own skin.' Listening to others I hear echoes of the same. We are wandering musical notes in search of a tune, and its very lack presses us on to seek a melody we have not yet discovered.

Our efforts to alleviate our restlessness and unease can create destructive havoc. Success is gratifying; control over circumstances is comforting; pleasure is enjoyable; gaining another's approval is affirming. Yet being dependent on any of these is also to be bound addictively. One shot is never enough; we soon need another to fill the void. Besides, objects such as these never quite do the trick. The gap we experience is not to do with the presence or absence of things. Their gain proves to be only a momentary release. What then, is this something we yearn for without wholly knowing its shape? It is meeting – it is love. It is the experience of being wholly loved, in and for oneself: the love that enables us to know and befriend who we are. But it is more. It is growing into the freedom to love: to move beyond self-absorption and share all we have and are with another with boundless generosity. This is when we sing; the plucked strings of our being find their melody.

At the heart of Christian revelation is the understanding that humankind is made in love for love; it is a pattern of relationship that has its source in God and that makes us whole. The lack we feel is the pain of separation from what we are made for but have yet to grow into. Augustine of Hippo, reflecting back on his own experience, saw the human heart as continually restless until it found its resting place in God.[4] We are question marks, seeking someone to understand us and so for the first time to understand ourselves. We are puzzle pieces, strangely shaped, searching for a place of belonging, trying this way and that way in the absence of a pattern; but all the time haunted by the sense there is a pattern, we do belong, there is logic to who we are. It is as if we carry within us the echo of a forgotten meeting – the lost memory of a love and life so rich that nothing else will satisfy – but we do not know who our lover is or where he is to be found. The Song of Songs expresses the heartache of this separation:

> Upon my bed at night
> I sought him whom my soul loves;
> I sought him, but found him not;
> I called him but he gave no answer.
> I will rise now and go about the city,
> in the streets and in the squares;
> I will seek him whom my soul loves.
> I sought him but found him not.[5]

---

4 Augustine of Hippo, *Confessions* Book 1, Chapter 1.
5 Song of Solomon 3.1–2

Yet for all the disturbance this unrest causes us it is also our hom-
ing device. If we stay with our restlessness it will begin to teach
us what we need. Our unease then becomes a motive force leading us to where life lies. In his poem *The Pulley*, George Herbert
imagines God's thoughts as he creates humankind. God pours out
his gifts one by one but stays his hand when it comes to granting
the gift of rest:

> Yet let him keep the rest (of his gifts)
> But keep them with repining restlesnesse:
> Let him be rich and wearie, that at least,
> If goodnesse leade him not, yet wearinesse
> May tosse him to my breast.

The first time I ever prayed from the depths of my being was
also the moment when I felt most intensely my emptiness and the
lack of anything within me capable of making me whole. Prayer
is when longing becomes purposeful seeking. One of the psalms
puts it this way:

> Out of the depths, I cry to you O Lord
> Lord, hear my voice!
> Let your ears be attentive
> to the voice of my supplications![6]

Out of the depths not only of our suffering but also the depths of
what we hope and long for; the height, length, depth and breadth
of who we might become if only the one we seek would answer.

The beginning is separation. I feel it today as I sit before my
computer willing words of truth and meaning to fill this page. I
feel it sometimes when the friends have gone, the work is done,
and there is nothing on the TV to distract me. I hear it within
the spaces between words of people who share their lives and
longings with me. And yet this separation seems in itself a form

---

6 Psalm 130.1–2

136

of meeting. I remember being given a drawing exercise: instead of trying to put down on paper the shape of the objects before us, we were encouraged to draw the space between and around them. I had never thought that way before: that the absence of what I could see had its own form every bit as real as what I could reach out and touch. What if, instead of fleeing the emptiness that breaks into our awareness so uncomfortably, we befriended it long enough to learn its shape: to know it not only as lack but also as presence; or at least the promise of presence? The wisdom of those early Christians who sought God in the desert was this: 'Go and sit in thy cell, and thy cell shall teach thee all things.'[7] It is hard not to flee when we are left with ourselves. What has silence and emptiness to teach us but our restlessness? But perhaps our restlessness has more to reveal to us than what we choose to cover it.

I greet him the days I meet him[8]

If we begin with separation then there are many ways in which we begin to experience meeting. Earlier Christian generations saw creation as a book where one with insight could read the works of the Lord; many still find themselves caught up in holy wonder in leafing through its pages. The song of a blackbird curls through the cold and grey of this May morning. Trees bud and break in a thousand colours of green. The scent of the pittosporum at night surprises me as I step from the street into our front garden. It is nature, science, biology and yet it also becomes conversation. What we see, touch and sense addresses us and invites our response. When I ask groups to share what experiences give them a sense of encountering God, most will begin with the beauty and surprise of the natural world: the sun breaking through clouds, the rhythmic beating of waves as they break upon the seashore

---

7 Helen Waddell, 1936, *The Desert Fathers*, London: Constable. The saying is attributed to Abba Moses.
8 Gerard Manley Hopkins, *The Wreck of the Deutschland*, stanza 5.

or the renewal of the earth on each return of spring. Others will point to more inward experiences: a sense of peace at the end of a prayer time; the gift of strength or of understanding when most needed; or the surprise of a creative spring of hope and purpose arising from a hidden well within.

A moment comes when in this way or that way we come to see how God is with us, and for this moment we know we are with God. Yet it is not our awareness that makes God present, as if God has to break into a world from which he is usually absent. His name, as given to Moses, is 'I AM'.[9] 'Where can I flee from your presence?' asks the psalmist, 'if I take the wings of the morning and settle at the farthest limits of the sea, even there your hand shall lead me.'[10] In darkness and light, in high place and low place, God 'is'. So rather than seeing those times of meeting as when God is present, we have to redraw our understanding. God is *always* with us, ever 'here' and 'now'; and sometimes we are aware of this presence and sometimes we are not. Moreover, the conscious experience of God is not something we can simply switch on or off. When we are otherwise engaged this perceived presence might interrupt us, and when we are actively seeking God it might elude our grasp. Our experience changes, but 'God with us' does not.

Sought and found

There is another way we might have to re-view the way we understand how our relationship with God is initiated and develops. Rather than all being dependent on the intensity of our search for God, the beginning, middle and end of this journey is God's search for us. What belongs to us is to recognize the seeker and to respond. This is entirely counter-cultural for me. The Christianity I received was a rather one-sided affair. I was to say my prayers, do good to others, be generous with what I had, avoid breaking

9 Exodus 3.14
10 Psalm 139

certain laid down rules and thereby show myself worthy of God's favour. Eternally that might mean heaven – if I managed to keep my standards up – and in life perhaps some form of blessing. It was a form of purposeful seeking but perhaps more driven by fear than love. I came at prayer with the same set of assumptions. If I concentrated enough, threw aside my distractions, got my technique right, then I would bring about God's presence. Meeting with God was something I had to make happen. However, my confidence was undermined by an underlying fear that prayer was one more of those things – like DIY, car maintenance, ballroom dancing, being the life and soul of the party – which I wasn't good at. Now I see how skewed those assumptions are. No prayer makes God present for the simple reason that God is already there. Prayer is attentiveness and openness to that presence which is always here and now, whether or not we are awake to it or are able to perceive it. Prayer matters, for it is consent on our side not only to the meeting but the transformation it will bring about in us. But we will not always *feel* met; sometimes this meeting will appear to us as separation.

Prayer is a purposeful seeking; but there is a surprise: all the while God is seeking us. The Gospels present this in time and place and in the context of particular people's lives. Levi, a tax collector, is sitting by the customs house and Jesus, seeing him, invites him to follow.[11] A Samaritan woman walks to the village well in the heat of the day and finds a stranger there who seems to know her unhappy life and promises her life-giving water.[12] Their Gospel is also ours. Jesus is always walking by, and ever waiting. He looks at us as no other looks. He invites us to stay in his company. John of the Cross put it this way:

This advice is very necessary, not only for all those who advance so prosperously but also for all others who seek their Beloved, I want to speak of it. In the first place it should be known that

---

11 Mark 2.15–17
12 John 4.1–15

if anyone is seeking God, the Beloved is seeking that person much more.[13]

Had John had the possibility of bold type and an increased font size I can imagine he would have taken every option open to him: 'this advice is very necessary . . . for all who seek . . . I want to speak of it.' Our seeking, our desire for relationship is only a pale shadow of God's active, resourceful and enduring longing for us. Simone Weil describes the surprise of this realization. Attracted and repelled by organized religion in equal measure, and with a deeply analytical and questioning mind, she had never seriously considered the possibility of personal and transformational religious experience. But then a day of 'meeting' came as she was reciting the lines of a poem she had come to value, *Love bade me welcome* by George Herbert:

> I discovered the poem of which I read you what is unfortunately a very inadequate translation. It is called *Love* . . . Often, at the culminating point of a violent headache, I would make myself say it over, concentrating all my attention upon it and clinging with all my soul to the tenderness it enshrines. I used to think I was merely reciting it as a beautiful poem, but without my knowing it the recitation had the power of a prayer. It was during one of these recitations that, as I told you, Christ himself came down and took possession of me.
>
> In my arguments about the insolubility of the problem of God I had never foreseen the possibility of a real contact, person to person, here below, between a human being and God. I had vaguely heard tell of things of this kind, but I had never believed in them . . . the accounts of apparitions rather put me off, like the miracles in the Gospel. Moreover, in this sudden possession of me by Christ, neither my sense nor my imagination

---

13 Kieran Kavanaugh and Otilio Rodriguez, 1991, 'Living Flame of Love', stanza 3.27–8 in *The Collected Works of John of the Cross*, translated and introduced by Kieran Kavanaugh and Otilio Rodriguez, Washington D.C.: ICS Publications.

had any part; I only felt in the midst of my suffering the presence of a love, like that which one can read in the smile on a
beloved face.[14]

Such meetings change us: life can never be the same again. Nor,
perhaps, do we want it to be, for like the woman whose thirst for
belonging could not be met by the well she walked to daily, or
Levi, dissatisfied by the money world he had given his life to, we
have been captivated by Love bidding us welcome.

Having been brought into an awareness of God's presence,
with the seeds of relationship planted, one might expect that
this tangible sense of meeting would become the ordinary. And
for many of us this is so, for at least much of the time. If we
purposefully seek God then, as Jesus promised, we shall find
him woven into the fabric of daily life. Of course there are dips:
times when our lives are not set towards God but drawn in other
directions. Our attention wanders. Sometimes we are too tired
and care-worn to be wholly present to anything or anyone. But
then we turn back to where we have begun to learn life is to be
found; or God graciously breaks through our dullness in a way
we have to try hard not to respond to. We feel separated for a
while but then meeting comes around again. But what are we
to make of the account of those whose lives are visibly turned
towards Christ and yet feel God has unexpectedly left them,
without note or explanation?

My God, My God

My God, my God, why have you forsaken me?
Why are you so far from helping me, from the words of my
groaning?
O my God, I cry by day, but you do not answer,
and by night, but find no rest . . .
Yet it was you who took me from the womb;

---

14 *Waiting for God* p. 27

you kept me safe in my mother's breast.
On you was I cast from my birth,
and since my mother bore me you have been my God.[15]

I have heard different explanations of Jesus' piercing cry from the anguish of the cross: 'My God, My God, why have you forsaken me?' Some hear despair and desperate isolation in its starkness. Some travel to the end of Psalm 22 with its affirmation of faith in God's goodness: 'He did not hide his face from me; he heard when I cried to him.' Perhaps, as with the psalm itself, both are true. Jesus feels abandoned by his Father and alone, and yet is wholly turned towards the enduring and compassionate presence he cannot feel. For Simone Weil the crucifixion captures the searing pain of separation; it is the moment of 'infinite distance between God and God', the 'supreme tearing apart', the 'agony beyond all others' and it is also the 'marvel of love'.[16] This is no pretend anguish – it is loss in its most raw form. And yet here, Jesus' being is set towards his Father. In feeling, Jesus has never been further away; in will and desire, he has never been closer. For Simone Weil this togetherness in being apart is not only between humankind and God but between 'God and God':

> Lovers or friends desire two things. The one is to love each other so much that they enter into each other and make one being. The other is to love each other so much that, with half the globe between them, their union will not be diminished in the slightest degree. All that humanity vainly desires here below is perfectly realised in God.[17]

Because 'no other could do it', Christ himself 'went to the greatest possible distance, the infinite distance'. Here separation and meeting sound together 'like two notes separate yet melting into

15 Psalm 22.1–2, 9–10
16 *Waiting for God* p. 72
17 *Waiting for God* p. 84

one, like pure and heart-rending harmony.'[18] Yet even if Christ has inhabited and transformed the pain of separation within our experience of meeting with God, the question is still not answered: why do we suffer so? Why, if God desires relationship and continually seeks us out, do those who seek him find him so elusive?

A grown-up love

I remember losing my temper over a game of Monopoly. I was probably only about seven at the time and the horror of landing on a particularly large constellation of houses and hotels and so losing all my money was more than I could cope with. I guess that when I had played the game previously my older brother and sister had been kind to me, miscounting the turn of the dice so that I picked up my £200 for 'passing go' and avoided any great harm. This time, however, they decided I was old enough to play the game as it really was, and I didn't like it. They had lured me into enjoying the game and then, when I was feeling that nothing but good could happen to me, they let me have it. It was time for me to grow up.

It seems hardly appropriate to draw parallels between a game based on the accumulation of money and the growth of relationship with God. The latter is not a game; there are no rules set up to trip the unwary. Yet there are connections. We make assumptions that seem safe at first but prove not to stand up to reality. God will answer our prayer, reward us with a sense of wellbeing, and assure us of his presence and help. After all God cares for us, so we are told, and God is faithful and unchanging. So when we pray and feel nothing, or when events continue to turn against us no matter how hard we entreat God's help, our expectations are dashed; we feel confused and let down. But our understanding of how the relationship works was flawed from the beginning. We

18 *Waiting for God* p. 82–3

came to an analysis that was easy and convenient for us but never resembled the reality.

I did play Monopoly again and as years went by understood more of its nuances. I learnt to enjoy the challenge of putting into effect whatever tactical awareness I had gathered. The previous version, where I could never fail and things would always turn out my way, would have soon begun to feel limited. But the process of moving from one understanding to another was not easy and I can't say I ever learnt to enjoy landing on Mayfair and paying the price. A limited relationship moves towards one based on the truth of the two parties involved. It is uncomfortable, challenging, but richer and deeper than what preceded it. The metaphor runs dry. I no longer play Monopoly and it does not really matter that this is so. But I am still caught in relationship with God and it is more than a game. It is the source of my life.

Perhaps hide and seek is a better analogy, based on what many experience. No sooner has God appeared, stirring our interest and desire, than he moves out of view and beyond our reach. As time goes by we might begin to believe that God has lost interest in us and that his love is a sham. But such inconstancy in love is the one thing impossible for God – a contradiction with his very nature. 'I call you friends', Jesus tells his disciples,[19] and this friendship is expressed in God's continual labour for us as one who comes alongside, creates, heals and unifies. But will this friendship always be expressed in ways we find convenient? We cannot simply plug God in and get a resultant shock of peace and wellbeing: 'All is well with me and I feel it instantly.' We are summoned to a grown-up love capable of going with, but also transcending, feeling. The absence of reward is not a mean way of testing us ('prove that you love me!'). Instead it is a deeper calling forth of our capacity for self-gift – an expansion of the heart – that also creates the room within to receive more.

We experience a pale shadow of this when we fall in love. It is wonderful to fall in love. Meeting moves on to life-long partnership

19 John 15.15

in this way. The power of the attraction we are caught up in enables us to make sacrifices for the other person and not even think of the cost. For the right person we are prepared to risk all, and it seems easy, carried as we are by the wave of our desire to be one with this person who fills our thoughts. After some time the relationship 'settles down'; the colours are less vivid, the excitement less intoxicating, and even a sense of routine begins to develop. The weekly shop might once have felt blissful in the company of our beloved but the sensation is unlikely to last forever. Now we have to choose this commitment we have made where once it might have felt impossible to do anything otherwise. Love becomes something we practise in small and daily actions rather than a feeling that carries all before it. We begin to recognize the reality of 'richer and poorer, better and worse, in sickness and in health'. The danger might be that we withdraw, piece by piece, the commitment we have made. Something has been lost – but it is not love; love only takes its true form now, if only we stay with the choice to be daily generous with one another. And then a moment comes when we are caught in the sensation of 'being in love' again. It might be that the experience is less dramatic, but we see it goes deeper too. Lives are now interwoven. We love not the idea of the beloved but their reality, and grasp that we are loved in the same way. We have less need to pretend, less to fear. There is the intensity of meeting, and the separation from that intensity, but both are one love; and without some diminishment in the sheer pleasure in being with the other, the commitment could not work deeper.

In her early life Thérèse of Lisieux felt Christ intimately close to her; he was the delight of her life and her constant friend and companion. Such tangible and generous love led her to a dedicated life of seeking and serving her Lord within the Carmelite order. And then it all changed. Christ was gone and she was left alone. Writing to her 'spiritual mother', the Prioress of her community, Thérèse explained that whilst it must seem from the verses she wrote that she was 'a soul filled with consolations' and that 'the veil of faith' was 'almost torn aside', her inward reality was that the veil had become 'a wall' reaching up to heaven and covering 'the starry firmament':

When I sing of the happiness of heaven and of the eternal possession of God I feel no joy in this, for I sing simply what I WANT TO BELIEVE. It is true that at times a very small ray of the sun comes to illumine my darkness and then the trial ceases for an instant, but afterwards the memory of this ray, instead of causing me joy, makes my darkness even more dense.[20]

And yet feeling so far removed from the presence of God that once gave her such joy, Therese wants one thing: 'I no longer have any great desires except that of loving to the point of love.'[21]

This desire to love is not something so rarefied and dreamy that it is of no earthly use. Instead what Thérèse experiences is that even though God seems absent, her capacity to be generous in her relationships with those around her – including those she naturally finds most difficult – grows larger. She describes how within the close-knit community there is a sister who had the ability of displeasing her in everything: 'in her ways, her words, her character, everything'. Accordingly she set herself to seek her out when she had opportunity and offer her whatever service she could. Sometimes the struggle to overcome her antipathy became too much and she ran away 'like a deserter'. The sister, absolutely unaware of Thérèse's feelings for her, at one point asks her, 'Sister Thérèse of the Child Jesus, what attracts you so much towards me; every time I look at you I see you smile?'[22] The point of the story is not that Thérèse overcame her feelings to such an extent that she came to enjoy the company of her sister – she never did – but that she wanted to love her for who she was, and found she was able to express a care for her in practice, and that this took place in a time when she felt far apart from Christ. Being willing to give ourselves to God when God seems absent is the birth of a free and unbounded love. This love is not something we manufacture;

20 *Story of a Soul, The Autobiography of St. Thérèse of Lisieux*, Third Edition translated from the original manuscript by John Clarke O.C.D., ICS Publications, Washington DC, 1996, p. 214.
21 *Story of a Soul*, p. 214
22 *Story of a Soul*, p. 222–3

rather it begins to flow through us as we have the largeness of spirit to trust in a love we cannot feel, and to consent to return the gift of ourselves even when any reward for this is removed. The divine love we thus make room for expresses itself in all our relationships; it becomes an integral part of our way of being. But at the level of our feelings we will often continue to struggle, because this love is a gift and not our possession.

For Simone Weil this loving in and through the affliction of separation is a grown-up love that mirrors and expresses the love that God is: a wholly generous self-giving. Requiring nothing in return God goes in search of us:

> The infinity of space and time separates us from God. How are we to seek for him? How are we to go towards him? . . . We cannot take a step towards the heavens; God crosses the universe and comes to us.[23]

If we consent to receive him then 'God puts a little seed in us and he goes away again.' But this seed of love so planted in us only grows to maturity through 'pulling up the weeds, cutting the couch grass'.[24] It hurts to learn to love more than we do. To love with the love that God is, requires us to go beyond ourselves, and to do so freely, and entirely for the other:

> A day comes when the soul belongs to God, when it not only consents to love but when truly and effectively it loves. Then in its turn it must cross the universe to go to God. The soul does not love like a creature with created love. The love within it is divine, uncreated; for it is the love of God for God which is passing through it.[25]

The letter to the Ephesians tells the story in a different way. Our inner being is to be strengthened through the Spirit so that Christ

---

23 *Waiting for God*, p. 91
24 *Waiting for God*, p. 72–3
25 *Waiting for God*, p. 80

may dwell in our hearts. Then, 'rooted and grounded in love' we begin to comprehend the 'breadth, and length and height and depth' of the love of Christ and become 'filled with all the fullness of God'.[26] It sounds comforting; yet how else are we going to be able to receive and express the fullness of God without being stretched and pulled? God needs so much room. Within the experience of meeting, when all that we need and desire is given and we feel that this is so, a small love will do. But in separation, when there is nothing and no one to greet us, love moves into a new territory: self-giving. Only in this way do we gain the velocity to escape the orbit of our self-absorption.

Another gravity

The rhythm of meeting and separation (if rhythm is a term that can be used for a pattern so unpredictable and troubling) is held within a process of the deepening of relationship. Meeting intensifies rather than stems longing. We have a sense now of what it is we have been missing for so long. John of the Cross sees God continually drawing us towards himself. As we respond the pull grows stronger until we find ourselves 'rushing towards God as rapidly as a falling stone when nearing its centre.' We are caught in the force field of another gravity, moving us into the heart of God, that is also our centre and where our longing finds its natural home. We are like 'a sketch or the first draft of a drawing' calling out to the artist to 'finish the painting and image'. We glimpse something of what this artist is creating within, but sense there is so much more we do not know, and cannot be, except that his labour continues. We are 'like wax in which an impression, though being made, is not yet complete'. How will this impression of meeting find its expression in the person we become? There is recognition of God's work within us and the more we can be, but then we are faced with how far we lie from this reality. We sense God's intimate presence in a graced moment, but then the day

---

26 Ephesians 3.14–21

moves on and we no longer know we walk in the light of his face. There is meeting and there is separation.[27]

One of the difficult truths we learn is that love – like faith and hope – is not primarily a sensation, but a choice. We do not always feel love or loved but we give of ourselves anyway. Love is a matter of orientation – a way we set ourselves to face life. If this is so, how is love any different from duty? There is overlap between the two. Both ask faithfulness and self-discipline and must work in the absence of encouragement. The following of duty, however, may tend to what destroys as much as to what gives life; it may be moved by fear or coercion. Love is the being and activity of God, always creative and unifying; it is always a choice and it is never to do with fear. To the degree we love, God lives in us and we live in God. To say that love is not primarily a sensation is not to despise or dismiss feeling; it is simply to state that feeling comes and goes, and though we welcome it gladly whenever it is present we cannot count on it. As disconcerting as this truth is, it might also begin to be liberating. Prayer does not have to produce a resultant inner peace or new insight to be worthwhile; it becomes a choice to be with God irrespective of the outcome. We do not have to sift the evidence to see whether or not we are in God's favour; we rest in this as a given. We are not limited by the need of reward or acknowledgement before we give of ourselves to another; we are free to be generous at any time. The foundation for the response of love is trust that God's being and activity is set towards us, and always will be, and always was, long before we ever thought of making any return.

Remembering meeting

There are days of meeting and perhaps they are given to us to help us through the days of separation. I remember sitting on a bright

---

27 The images in this paragraph are taken from Kavanaugh and Rodriguez, 1991, *The Collected Works of John of the Cross*, 'The Spiritual Canticle', stanza 12.1.

May morning on a Welsh hillside, surrounded by contented sheep. The sun warmed the coldness in my body and spirit through. Across the valley I could rest my gaze on the distant mountains of Snowdonia, or look below to a patchwork of fields. I needed to be no one other than who I was and nowhere other than this place – for that morning at least. But on the next day I would leave to return to London, to demands I struggled to meet and streets too cramped by buildings for horizons. I felt God saying to me: 'Today you feel my presence and the warmth of my love; soon you will leave here and go to a very different place; but even if you don't feel it or see it, the presence and the love you feel today will always be with you.' Years have gone by since. But on over-crowded days, when my anxieties gather to keep me company, and the presence of God seems beyond my grasp, I know that moment on the mountain continues to exist and always will. Before his death Jesus gave his disciples words to see them through days of separation:

A little while, and you will no longer see me, and again a little while, and you will see me . . . You will weep and mourn . . . you will have pain, but your pain will turn into joy . . . I will see you again, and your hearts shall rejoice, and no one will take your joy from you.[28]

The resurrection narratives speak not so much of meeting after separation but of a new reality where meeting and separation are intertwined within our experience. Mary Magdalene weeps in the garden where Jesus was laid. Peter and his companions try to put out of their minds the trauma of the death of their friend by return-ing to their fishing. Two companions take the long road home to Emmaus, mourning the loss of their dream. Recognition of a new reality comes in a moment: the calling of a name, an unexpected haul of fish, the familiar movement of a stranger breaking bread. The risen Jesus meets them, and meets us, at the unanticipated

28 John 16.17–22

moment and within the dark as well as the light of our days. We greet him not so much in the removal of our troubles but as he breaks bread with us within them.

And then the moment is gone. Mary Magdalene cannot hold on to Jesus and we cannot grasp this Easter Day experience or make it happen again at our will. But also the moment is not gone; it dwells in the storehouse of our memory. We can ponder it, returning to that time when difficulty envelops us and we can no longer see our way. Hope has found a home within, and if we search deeply enough it will find us again.

For reflection:

1] We meet God in the ordinary and everyday: in those moments when we become aware. When have you met God? As a memory of a time, recent or past, comes to mind, write down a few words that express the character of that experience. Then allow another memory to come in, and again write a word or words to note that time. Continue the same process until you have filled up your page or come to a natural pause. Now look through what you have written. What feelings and thoughts arise in you? You may find yourself wanting to express some of these to God, or being drawn into some particular memory that seems significant for this time.

2] John of the Cross affirmed that if anyone is seeking God, God is seeking that person much more. Are there any ways in which you sense God seeking you? How will you respond?

3] *Imaginative contemplation*: This is a way of prayer that uses the imagination to enter into a Gospel passage, allowing it to interact with the place where we are. It may take a little time to settle into this way of prayer. Take your time and relax: the fruit of this prayer is in God's gift rather than dependent on the strength of your powers of imagination!

Choose a Gospel passage that describes a meeting between Jesus and another person. Some examples are given in this chapter: Mary

Magdalene meeting Jesus in the garden (John 20.1–18); Peter and his companions meeting Jesus on the lake shore (John 21.1–19); the disciples on the road to Emmaus (Luke 24.13–35).

- Make yourself at home in the presence of God. You may find it helps to spend a few minutes stilling yourself down, giving your attention to what you can hear around you, or becoming aware of the rhythm of your breathing.
- Bring to God what it is you are seeking today, for example a deeper awareness of his presence, guidance in a decision you are making, or greater freedom to be able to let go to God. Ask God to help you to pray with openness and generosity of spirit.
- Read the bible passage through a couple of times slowly and reflectively.
- Put the Bible down, and in your imagination set the scene described in the passage. The setting might be similar to that described in the Bible, or you may find the setting changes to one that connects in some way with your past/present experience.
- Use all your senses. What can you see, hear, feel, taste, or smell?
- Now put yourself into the story. Who are you? A central character or someone observing from the sidelines?
- Let the scene unfold in its own way. The story may stick closely to what you read in the Gospel or take on a life of its own; rather than fight this, trust that it's OK, and that this is the story that it is important for you to attend to today.
- You may find yourself wanting to talk to Jesus as the story unfolds or to ask him a question; or that Jesus speaks to you. It may be that you engage with another person in the scene.
- Be aware of your own feelings and responses as you pray through the passage.
- When you have finished, look back over the prayer. Remember how you reacted and felt at different points. What seems to you significant? Did anything surprise you? Ponder what this might be saying to you, asking God to help you see and understand.

- Spend some time in prayer with God sharing your thoughts, feelings and needs.

You may find it helpful to repeat the prayer at another time, returning to those points where you were conscious of being moved in some way.

9

Fruit from the Tree

O King of the Friday,
Whose limbs were stretched on the cross;
O Lord who did suffer the bruises, the wounds, the loss;
We stretch ourselves beneath the shield of thy might.
Some fruit from the tree of thy passion
Fall on us this night![1]

How do we meet suffering, whatever its cause might be? The beginning is to *meet* it, rather than seek to deny its existence or blame someone that it has come our way. Yes, we need to give vent to our feelings, but ultimately life owes us no favours and must be faced as it is, rather than as it should have been.

Anyone who spends time listening to people tell their life stories will come to marvel at humankind's resilience; our instinct for survival is remarkably strong. But though we might survive, the experience will have changed us in some way: made us more wary or more open, more defensive or more compassionate, more damaged or more whole. Beyond survival we are challenged to find a means of integrating our difficult experiences into our story so that they begin to work creatively rather than destructively. As we come through pain are we left with a legacy of fear and bitterness, or with a greater capacity to trust and to forgive? Do we put up our defences to keep future threats at bay, or find within ourselves more hospitable space where we can offer others shelter? Are we more alive to the beautiful within the ordinary, and the giftedness

---

1 An ancient Irish Prayer, author unknown.

of existence, or less so? Suffering is a considerable test of our spirit. But we are not alone. There is fruit from the tree of Christ's Passion. His presence in our present – whatever joy or sorrow this moment holds – has the capacity to turn what is death-dealing into the life-giving. There is fruit, and it is for our growth.

Today I went into a church and sat for a while. Before me were two crosses. One large cross of polished brass shone brightly over the entrance to the sanctuary, reflecting the light from the windows. A smaller wooden cross, bearing the image of the crucified Christ, hung on the wall by the pulpit. The empty cross, flinging out the reflection of the sun, proclaimed resurrection. The cross is empty; Christ has risen; suffering and death are overcome. The wooden cross had Christ suffering still, his arms outstretched and pinioned into our pain. Side by side, they told different stories; which was to be believed?

The life, death and rising of Christ happened within moments of time – moments that can be measured and that come and then go. One event follows another. In his humanity this is how Jesus lived his life, his body changing as years went by; his death coming when he was still a young man. But as God with us, Jesus dwells in the 'now' that is also eternity; past and future gathered into a boundless present. In this now, Christ still suffers on the cross, hurting and questioning, inhabiting our difficulties. And in this now he rises, and we in him also rise.

In the Gospel of John, as Jesus dies he gives up his spirit; and when a soldier pierces his body with a lance, blood and water flow from his side.[2] The passage, as usual in John's writing, is rich in symbolism. Jesus had promised that 'rivers of living water' – the very life-giving Spirit of God – would flow from the believer's heart.[3] Earlier in John's account, Jesus had identified his body as the true Temple, the dwelling-place of God.[4] Another biblical echo can be heard: the vision of the prophet Ezekiel who sees a mighty stream flowing from the Temple. Wherever the river flows, life

2 John 19.30–4
3 John 7.38
4 John 2.18–21

flourishes; bitter salt water becomes fresh. On the banks of the river grow trees whose fruit is for food and whose leaves are for healing.[5] So what, according to John, is happening as Jesus dies? Is it death, defeat and sadness, or the giving of life, new beginnings and joy? Is this Good Friday, Easter Day or Pentecost, or all three at one and the same time, though we see only part of the reality? As we seek God, are all our dyings also resurrections, all our endings also new beginnings, all our losing, the being found by one who loves us beyond all telling?

Our struggling, anguish and disorientation are real; we bend beneath their weight. Christianity faces full-square the messy, the awkward and the difficult. The crucifix does not deny the empty cross. Instead it affirms that here, amidst the debris and destruction, the hurt and the harm, here – where we most need it – is where resurrection happens. We do not have to choose between empty cross and crucifix. Nor do we have to deny our pain in order to affirm our faith in the resurrection, or cling to suffering as all-enveloping reality. We can doubt and choose to trust, struggle against God yet not let go, feel far away from God and still believe we are intimately held.

After all, as we have seen, the search for God is full of contradictions. The almighty one we seek comes naked and dependent into the world as a baby. The one beyond time is spoken in a moment of time. The creator of all things is destroyed by human violence. The cross – a symbol of cruelty and death – becomes a symbol of everlasting kindness and hope. Losing leads to finding and letting go to receiving. The Lord is revealed as servant, the poor are most rich and the sinner finds warmth and welcome.

A shelter for sorrow

It is time to call one last witness to help gather what has been explored over these chapters. Etty Hillesum did not set out to confront suffering; it emerged from her peripheral vision as the

---

5 Ezekiel 47.1–12

FRUIT FROM THE TREE

familiar life she had known was swept away. Instead she wanted to find a way of living her life at greater depth, and fulfilling the draw she had long felt within to be a writer. She was aware that her inner life lacked order; she recognized she could be all over the place and this sometimes caused her distress. Her personal relationships could be chaotic too. She had a physical relationship with the widower to whom she was housekeeper and later with the person who acted as mentor for her search for a more integrated and purposeful life. It was an accident of history that she began this journey as a young woman of Jewish descent in Nazi-occupied Holland. Her journal traces the growing tide of oppression almost incidentally at first, as the growing list of limitations placed on the freedom of movement of Jews began to make small inroads on her pattern of life. As the restrictions grew more severe, and rumours spread about evils done elsewhere, the question of how to respond to this cruelty and the suffering it brought moved towards the forefront of her mind. But even with her 'two feet . . . planted on the hardest soil of harshest reality'[6] she knew the personal question of how to make the best of her life remained important; suffering became the context within which she had to find her answer.

At an early stage Etty came to see that alongside the discipline of physical exercise she needed to become more focused in mind and in spirit. Keeping a journal was one means of paying attention to her inner life; another was the practice of daily meditation. She described this as listening to her 'inner voice', making herself 'a vast empty plain' so that 'something of "God"' could enter, and 'something of "Love" too.'[7] Giving generous space for her inner being and for God became important for another reason. She came to see that the external conflicts all too present in her outer world had their origin and resolution in the inner world of each human being. She must put her inner space at the service of

---

6 Quotations from Etty Hillesum are taken from: Etty Hillesum, 1999, *An Interrupted Life: the Diaries and Letters of Etty Hillesum 1941–43*, London: Persephone Books. This quotations is from page 216.

7 p. 33

the problems of her time and 'not run away'.[8] Would she respond to aggression with hatred? Or could she find it within herself to recognize the common frailty we share that makes some strike out in anger or fear, and so not give up on her fellow human beings? Would she cower away from the unknown, or choose to remain receptive and trusting? Etty understood that the way she met her own struggles had significance beyond the orbit of her one small life. She was careful to say that she had not risen to such a high spiritual plain that sorrow and evil deeds did not affect her. She could still be overcome with sadness; at times she rebelled, and refused to acquiesce to the course of events. She describes her 'moral indignation' at the cruel workings of the Nazi regime.[9] And yet she understood that closing life down through responding with hatred and fear only further diminishes us; events had become 'too overwhelming and demonic to be stemmed with personal resentment or bitterness.'[10] What she began to glimpse was a middle road between fight and flight. Instead of clinging to difficult events she saw that she must allow them to pass through her, 'like life itself, as a broad eternal stream . . . they become part of that stream and life continues.' Instead of running away from grief, or seeking relief for her feelings through hatred, she must give her sorrow 'all the space and shelter' within her that was due. Then we come to a place where we are able to say, 'life is beautiful and so rich. So beautiful and so rich that it makes you want to believe in God.'[11]

Etty felt that people of her time had lost the knowledge of how to meet difficulty as part of life. She noted in her journal, 'We in the West don't understand the art of suffering and experience a thousand fears instead. We cease to be alive, being full of fear, bitterness, hatred and despair.'[12] The way forward, she suggested, was to accept death as part of life – the final death that brings an

---

8 p. 37–8
9 p. 216
10 p. 216
11 p. 118–19
12 p. 186

end to life, but also the lesser deaths of the daily hardships that come our way.[13] It was a matter of 'living from minute to minute and taking suffering into the bargain.'[14] In accepting these deaths, we also become fully alive to the gift and beauty of life. In her mind she was 'with the hungry and ill-treated and dying every day', but also present to 'the jasmine and . . . that piece of sky beyond my window.'[15] She pondered the paradox of continuing to find life meaningful in the context of knowing that the Nazis' desire for her and her friends was 'total destruction'.[16]

In a prayer in her journal written on a Sunday morning, Etty talked with God about 'scene after scene of human suffering' that passed through her mind. She knew there would be no divine intervention to turn back the inevitable tide of evil:

> One thing is becoming increasingly clear to me: that You cannot help us; that we must help You to help ourselves. And that is all that we can manage these days and also all that really matters. Alas, there doesn't seem to be much You Yourself can do about our circumstances, about our lives. Neither do I hold You responsible. You cannot help us, but we must help You and defend your dwelling place inside us to the last.[17]

God has let go of his creation; and yet God has come alongside, making his home in the human heart, inviting us to make our home in his. God is within, and inside that room nothing is lost, even though in time and place all seems lost. Even though the jasmine behind her house that has given her so much pleasure has been ruined by the rain, inside her 'the jasmine continues to blossom undisturbed, as profusely and delicately as it ever did. And it spreads its scent round the House in which You dwell, O God.'[18]

---

13 p. 190
14 p. 186
15 p. 186
16 p. 188
17 p. 217–18
18 p. 219

I began by suggesting that Etty Hillesum did not set out to confront suffering, but to know who she was. She might have got to that end in another way had she been born in another time and place. But as it was, suffering brought the fruit she sought. This was down to her openness to meet it, but also to the room she made within for God, who chooses human brokenness as the place of his dwelling. In their different ways each of the images used in this book says something of how God meets us within the difficulty we experience, and something of what shape of response enables us to co-operate with this active and compassionate presence. Etty Hillesum's dwelling place of God within was a touching-place with eternity, a shelter where sorrows could be received and find new existence as fruit. She had to consent to the building of this shelter and commit herself to the maintenance of this holy space. Then, she believed, the reality of suffering was 'always fruitful', capable of turning a life into 'a precious thing.'[19]

Gathering the fruit

Fruit takes its own time to grow. We can help create the conditions where a harvest is more likely to happen – for instance by clearing smothering weeds or feeding the soil – but the development of the fruit itself is not entirely in our hands. The process is mysterious, wonderful – and frustrating if we are in a hurry. In some instances it seems as if there is scarcely a break between the flower forming and fading and the fruit emerging; but in others long months pass by with little apparent movement. Hadewijch saw herself as the hazel tree that sends out its catkins in the bleak months of winter, and has to wait until autumn begins for the fruit to be ripe. As we work through difficulties we may have to be patient to see any benefit from our experience. There will be a harvest if we remain open to its coming.

It is with this thought in mind that I will now provide a brief reminder of the imagery we have explored. As you read through, you

---

19 p. 269

may already recognize the fruit of your experience that has taken this form; but it may be you are still waiting, and any thought of anything positive emerging from what you are going through seems far from where you are. Fruit takes its own time to grow; it will not be rushed. But grow it will, if we meet the difficult and painful with whatever courage and honesty we can muster, and for the rest, put our trust in the presence and activity of God.

To say that suffering is part of life is not to invite passive resignation. John of the Cross found a way of escaping the dark confinement of his prison cell. But still he was grateful for what he had discovered there: that being out of control of our circumstances creates the opportunity for a larger movement of trust. How he must have welcomed the feel of the wind and sun upon his face on finally gaining his freedom; how liberating to look out on wide horizons after the cramp of daily pacing a handful of space! And yet a prison cell was where he had learnt to give God room and let himself be drawn into the spaciousness of the receiving and giving of love. The real imprisonment, he discovered, was not to trust and so be left in the confines of fear. Night invites us to stay with what we can neither wholly control nor comprehend and so receive its gift to us, rather than wear ourselves out in the attempt to reduce life and people to something that fits into the particular box of our personal expectation and need. In the daytime of living as a free man, John never forgot that it was through night that he found his true liberty in allowing himself to be taken deeper into God. Only those willing not to see and not to know will come to perceive and to understand.

It is during a night crossing of a river that Jacob finds himself wrestling with God. One notion of faith has the believer living in untroubled certainty, never doubting for a moment his sure place in God's care, nor needing to question why things happen as they do. But I do question, and I do doubt, and I suspect you do too. If our relationship with God is to mean anything then it has to be marked by honesty. Our feelings are real and they need expression. Anger and frustration can be prayer as much as thankfulness or praise. Psalm 23, with its image of a cup overflowing with the experience of the kindness and care of God within adversity, sits side by side with the pained cry of Psalm 22: 'Why have you forsaken me?' Job refuses the easy answers of his friends. Struggle has its rightful place. Not to question would be not to care. Jacob will not let go, but nor will the stranger he wrestles with release him. Even as the struggle intensifies the bond of relationship is strengthening. The contest takes place at a crossing point – a ford not just between one side of a river and the other but also between an old reality and a new one. Jacob moves on, limping but blessed; the bearer of a new name. We bear the honourable wounds of our struggles, but also their blessings. Our names are revealed to us; we know more of who we are, and more of the one we have wrestled with. We cross the river enriched for the next stage of our journey.

We might not immediately identify someone as gentle and compassionate as Julian of Norwich as a Jacob who struggles with God, and yet closer reading of her work shows how persistent she is in wrestling with questions whose answers elude her. She will not be content until she finds a way to reconcile the love of God with the destructiveness evident within his creation. Suffering enters her life in the pain of those she counsels, the rumours of war, famine and evil deeds that reach into her anchorhold, and in the fluctuations within her own temperament. We fall so far and in our pain and confusion strike out against others and ourselves. 'All will be well' is not good enough for her; she wants to know how the broken will be made whole and where God is within this process. What she comes to understand is that God has anticipated our falling by his chosen descent into our humanity in Christ. The servant, Adam, everyone, is joined on the ground by the servant Christ who becomes the means of Adam's rising. We never fall out of the love of God. Rather than drown in the misery of our failings we look at God who can do no other than have compassion on us, and who continually labours to make all manner of things well. The wounded world is wound with mercy.

We live within the rhythm of seasons. We are not so far removed from movements within the natural world as twenty-first-century minds might imagine. We too have had our beginning and will have our end. Our life, which seems of such consequence to us, will pass from memory, flourishing for its moment only for the wind to pass over it and its place to know it no more.[20] Is the shortness of our life a tragedy, or does knowledge of this begin to deliver us from anxiety? There are so many things you and I worry about that are of little consequence. What matters is to be what we can be and give what we can give for this brief span, as every flower inhabits its moment and its ground to the full. And the paradox is that the now and here is also time without boundary. We enter the God-life of eternity in the point of time and space when we are wholly alive and aware.

Each season brings its challenge. Spring comes with lengthening day and leaf-green light. Do we dare overcome our lethargy and lack of belief and allow God to renew us once more? How hard to leave behind comfortable decay and push new shoots through into the still-cool day. Summer bids us to live generously, allowing the fullness of our being to be seen and shared in flower and fruit. But there are days of drought when we call out to the Lord of Life to send our roots rain. Autumn invites us to let go, for only then will the seeds of another springtime be broken open by frost and rain. But it is hard to let go of what we have invested in and what has become dear to us. Will anything be left for us? Will what we have released return to us in some way? Winter is long. The light is low. Nothing seems to grow. How hard it is to wait, for our life to lie dormant. We cannot see the work of renewal that begins underground. How very hard to wait.

We enter the dance of these different movements time after time without ever mastering the steps; they continue to surprise us. We move against the rhythm and find ourselves wrenched unwillingly into place. And then we begin to move again, drawing deeper into God and to where our own life lies.

Those who wander in a wilderness do not know where they are going nor why the path has led them into this desolate land. Hindsight might know it as the place of passage between one reality that was and another that is to be, but those who walk here

---

20 Psalm 103.15–16

only see its limitless horizons. Their quest is framed in questions: 'When will I regain the meaning my life once had? Is there any end to this experience that so strips me bare? Who will tell me who I am and where I belong?' The searching seems to bring them no nearer to finding what they are looking for. As its name suggests, the wilderness is untamed; it will not be managed and will never be comfortable. Here they are hounded by the wild beasts of their needs, drives and insecurities. They have no means of escaping themselves; the usual diversions do not work here. Yet as Williams' great hymn reminds us, this wild place is also the place of encounter with the living God. Illusions fall away to leave space for meeting. We know ourselves in the raw, rather than through the carefully presented face that once defended us from being known by others, and from knowing ourselves. Our reality helps us be open to God's reality. We might begin to glimpse that though incapable of managing our future we are held within uncertainty by a powerful and guiding hand. We cannot provide what we need to sustain us, but God gifts us with daily bread from the skies. At our most thirsty we discover a crystal fountain of life-giving water welling up from within. We do not know our way and sometimes the degree of our confusion overwhelms us, but we gradually learn to recognize the cloud and the fiery pillar that assure us that there is after all a path to be followed and a meaning to this journey. Whilst the wilderness seems the place where all that was once known and counted on falls apart, it is in truth the place of our formation and integration. It is the locus of relationship, where in the presence of I AM we begin to know who we are.

In many ways the Ignatian *Spiritual Exercises* parallel this wilderness experience. Those who enter them freely discover how imprisoned we human beings are. We have our inner slave-drivers, who keep us in a place of fear masked as security. We face the wrong way, led by our need to keep life safe, to shut out the prospect of hurt and to maintain control. Without knowing that we are doing so, we imprison our true selves, wrapping our days in self-induced mediocrity. Ignatius' guidance helps those who desire to align their lives towards what is true and life-giving to recognize the voice of the Spirit. Instead of the familiar and loud prompt to defend ourselves against others, we learn to hear and respond to an invitation to trust. Hope seeps through into the pit of despair. The narrow confines of our self-absorption begin to open into the wide expanse of the receiving and giving of love. There is subtlety within the process. 'Consolation' does not always mean that which gives us immediate ease of heart, nor 'desolation' the presence of sorrow or difficulty. What matters is the direction of our travel: towards or away from living in faith, hope and love through relationship with God.

The 'consolation' of longing and yearning for God is known in the wonder and joy that comes with recognition of all that God is and does, and in the pained seeking of the one who feels restless and empty and knows that only God can meet her need. Meeting and separation are very different emotional experiences of the same abiding relationship. We seek and we find, but then on seeking once more are met only with the seemingly empty space where God once was. But the relationship does not die; it lives on in our continued turning towards the one whom we long for. The surprise breaks in that God has always sought us, and in those moments when we feel his absence, God still does. Meeting and separation, so different in how we receive them, are the drawing and calling of Love. On days when we feel presence and peace, and on days when we receive no more than the shape of where these gifts once lay, the bond of commitment deepens. We are summoned to a grown-up love, taking pleasure when pleasure comes but not dependent on its presence for the gift of our attentiveness to be shared. God invites no more than God freely gives. Love is an offering of ourselves we make for the other, not a grasping of what we desire, driven by need; but in the giving our lives are enriched and transformed.

Even if we are able to look back on a time of struggle and begin to be grateful for the part it has played in our growth we may still ask ourselves: 'but did it have to happen this way, with all this pain?' But this is the way it did happen, and this is how the fruit formed.

For reflection:

1] What fruit have you gained from past times of struggle and difficulty? Do you see any fruit forming within this current time? What form does it take?

2] Etty Hillesum wrote of how important it was for her to create and maintain a shelter within that housed God and that allowed sorrows to be received and given the space to become fruit. For her, keeping a journal and daily meditation helped to form this inner room. What practices will help you build your own shelter? How will you integrate these into your daily life?

3] Spend some time before an empty cross or crucifix, perhaps using the prayer at the beginning of the chapter as a way into your reflection and a means of closing it. What is your prayer to Christ? What are his words to you?

10

The Support We Need

It has been my privilege to accompany a number of people through difficult times, just as I have been gifted with people willing to give me space when I have been struggling. The emphasis of this book and of this chapter is on the spiritual dimension of suffering. Where is God within what we experience? How we are to find meaning in the face of events that are unplanned and unwanted? How do we meet these challenges so that they work for our growth rather than our disintegration? With these questions in mind I will focus here on the role of a spiritual director supporting someone travelling through difficulty. But much of what follows will apply equally to the work of a trusted friend or the one-off support given by a pastor to someone in their care. Whether we are a listening friend, a pastor or a spiritual director we are first and foremost a human being alongside another human being. The world is not divided into the helpers and helped. We all struggle sometimes and all need support. In accompanying another, we make a generous gift of our time and attentiveness. But on another day we will need the same gift of someone there for us.

The nature of spiritual direction

A spiritual director seeks to enable an individual to be attentive to the Spirit and to respond appropriately. This involves encouraging and equipping people to reflect on what is happening in outward events and inward thoughts and feelings. The director helps the person they are accompanying recognize and trust the 'voice' of the Spirit, and to distinguish it from drives, needs, fears, attitudes and beliefs that are destructive of self and others. Giving the 'directee' tools to discern the working of the Spirit is therefore central to the director's task: 'Where is God in all that I am experiencing, thinking and feeling, and what does this mean for the way I respond?'

It is often remarked that 'spiritual direction' is an unhelpful term, suggesting undue hierarchy in the relationship with one person telling the other what to do. But there is another way of befriending the term. The shared focus of this relationship does concern *direction* in the sense of life orientation. What guides us when making decisions within any journey is our understanding of where we want to get to. One way of expressing this goal from a Christian perspective is the living out of our full potential as human beings, in a way that brings life to others, through relationship with God. If this is the 'direction' then it is the Spirit that continually draws us along the path: taking us deeper into God, enabling us to be all that we can be and uniting us with Christ in loving service. We listen together to where the Spirit is leading and seek to discern how best to co-operate with this.

At the heart of the ministry of spiritual direction is hospitality; it is the creation of a safe space where someone can enter and rest for a while. Whilst at other times this person may need to put on a face, taking hold of their ongoing responsibilities, here they can be themselves. They can say it how it is without any fear of ridicule, rejection or meeting indifference. The willingness to be present and available for another is an immeasurable gift. Think for a moment of what happens when someone asks us how we are. Our stock response is 'I'm fine', irrespective of whether life is wonderful or totally falling apart. No other response is expected or wanted. Conversation is being made; it is not a real question. In the days of my naive youth I decided that when my colleague next asked me, 'How are you?' I would break rank and say how I really felt. The next morning she asked me how I was. 'To tell you the truth things have been a bit difficult', I responded. After a long pause she replied, 'What do you think about the agenda for next week's meeting?' I duly changed tack and told her it was a well-thought-out agenda and I was sure we'd have a good meeting. I don't blame her. I broke the rules, and it wasn't fair to spring a different script on her. But I felt more isolated than ever. The hospitality we offer is the willingness to *want* to know how the other is, not out of nosiness but because sometimes it makes a difference to have the space to say this. The places are rare where it is safe to lay down our roles and draw down our masks.

I wonder if my colleague turned to the agenda of next week's meeting not only because I had been inappropriately honest when I should have realized we were simply going through the formalities of greeting, but also because she felt out of her depth. One of the pressures we feel is that we have to come up with answers when people present us with questions. If someone says, 'I don't know why this is happening to me', how are we to respond if we too have no clue? One temptation is flight: to get out of the territory as quickly as we can for fear we make things worse. The other is to fill the pregnant pause of the question with a solution. On the receiving end this can feel even more difficult. Job's pain was added to by his companions' need to tell him exactly why he was suffering and what the remedy was. Sometimes there is no answer. The gift we can offer is not to turn away and to be willing to stay alongside as someone seeks the courage to live through the question.

There are times when it is given to us to sense what is going on and what a way forward might be. The wisdom of the 'cloud of witnesses' within this book is offered in this spirit. There are patterns that recur across different lives, and metaphors that help put a picture on experience. The voice of the Spirit of God has its particular sound and we need help to recognize this and co-operate with the Spirit's movement in our life. But what we share in terms of guidance we offer humbly and tentatively. We are not looking to dominate and control the other, or to impose our particular understanding. The relationship that matters will always be between the person and God, and our role is no more and no less than to encourage and enable that conversation. In the Old Testament we hear how the boy Samuel heard a voice calling to him in the night. He assumed it was that of his master, Eli, and ran to do his bidding. But Eli had not summoned him. Again Samuel heard someone call his name, and once more it was not Eli. Finally Eli understood that Samuel had been hearing God, but the boy did not understand that this was so because of his lack of experience. He told Samuel to lie back down and if he heard the voice again to reply, 'Speak Lord, your servant is listening.'[1] Eli directed Samuel to the conversation that mattered. His part was to help prepare Samuel to listen and to respond. So often we feel we have to provide a significant word of insight if not a definite answer, and whilst sometimes this is given to us to share, more often our part is to say: 'Go back and listen more until the answer becomes clear to you.'

Though our particular focus might be the spiritual content of the struggle someone is experiencing, our concern is always for the whole person. Someone might be unable to pray, or feel flat and stuck because they are physically worn out, or need a bit of fun in their life. Too much work and not enough play can wear away our spirit. Recreation can be re-creation. If someone is carrying too great a burden of responsibility, the immediate issue might be how they can put some of the weight down. God is practical. Jesus fed the 5000 because they were hungry. Elijah in despair was given cakes to eat and told to catch up on his sleep before his journey to the holy mountain. As one who cares, we try to see the whole person, and what they might need, and in what order.

When we are hurting, we sometimes turn against ourselves, beating ourselves up for not being able to cope better, or for making a mess of things; or driving ourselves to do more to make things right. More often than not what is needed is not more effort but more gentleness. It is wearing and wearying to struggle. We are in need of kindness – not hard labour. But it is difficult to release ourselves from punishment for our perceived weakness. We therefore stand in need of someone who will take our part and defend us against our own self-destructive instincts. Those who have helped me most have been those who encouraged me to welcome the person I am, and to render to myself that kindness

---

1 1 Samuel 3. 1–9

and patience that on better days I look to offer others. When a person alongside us persists in seeing our good, and believing in our future, we might eventually begin to believe it for ourselves. Their unwavering faith in us provides a mirror where we can begin to see ourselves as we are, and as God sees us. This is the best form of humility, neither puffing ourselves up nor putting ourselves down. We are all work in progress. We are weak; we do not have the power to resolve all our difficulties and we do get things wrong. But we are wanted, believed in and gifted with particular riches that find meaning when they are generously shared.

Putting a picture on our experience

What are the specific implications of the different images we have explored within this book? Perhaps a word of warning is needed at this point. The images are not neat boxes for us to pigeon-hole people, and thereby describe their condition and their remedy. Though differing in their emphasis they all point in the same direction, flowing as they do from our shared human condition and the activity of the same compassionate and resourceful God. We are looking through different windows at the same house, glimpsing another room within a larger whole. Each metaphor has something important to say to us, and a particular way of imagining what is happening to us and how we might respond may prove fitting and helpful for a particular time. But in the end they are metaphors and they have their limits. This person, in this place, is not summed up by seeing them as Jacob wrestling or as one walking in the dark. But what the metaphors can do is unlock the creative power of our imagination, now suggesting what lies at the heart of the struggle, and now hinting at the response needed at this point.

Those who guide others through night will encourage them to trust rather than fight the darkness. They bid those they accompany to take up the adventure of the beauty and richness that lies hidden in the dark, and to curb their instinct to flee to the safety of the nearest man-made light. I remember a mother taking her child on her first visit to a church. I unlocked the door and they stepped through from the daylight into the shadowy interior. The child tensed, unsure of what lay hidden there and wanting to go back outside. Instinctively her mother took her hand and together they took a few more steps in. After a while the child let go of her mother's hand and began to explore, taking in the patterned windows, the candles, the strange bench seats, the paintings on the wall. Soon she was running around freely, enjoying this new space and the treasures that lay hidden within. Perhaps what we need in the face of unfamiliar darkness is that metaphorical hand to help us stay with what we instinctively want to turn from.

Those who struggle with God, like Jacob, need to be given permission to say it how it is. We cannot make ourselves feel trustful and at peace amidst difficulty, if what is really going on for us is fear and turmoil. It is better to own what we feel, and then we can begin to listen to God. The relationship has to be real or it is nothing. Those in a difficult place may need reassurance that questions and doubts do not negate faith; in many ways they are the substance of faith. We can doubt and choose to trust, for faith is a choice we make rather than a feeling we ought to have. As one who listens and comes alongside we help create the space where a person can come before God as they are rather than as some idealized person they are not.

Those who feel themselves to have fallen and so find it hard to forgive themselves, have need of acceptance. Though falling hurts it does not separate us from God, who gladly chooses in Christ to fall into our difficulties, knowing we need that help. The encouragement we need is to avoid becoming overly self-absorbed and so mired in misery. Instead we need someone to remind us to gaze at God who bids us welcome. We can use this moment's insight into our need of God to help deepen the bond of relationship. Its fruit can be humility, our grounding in self-knowledge that enables us to relate to others and to life from the right place.

Each fresh challenge asks us: 'What time is it?' Is this the season to endure, patiently waiting whilst doing the little that remains in our power? Or is this a time to allow the new in our life to break through, displacing what was, and renewing our life in a way we could never have anticipated? Are we to let go or to take firmer hold? The ministry of spiritual direction centres on enabling people to discern and then co-operate with the movement of the Spirit. What was an appropriate response once may not be helpful now. Both director and directee must be open and attentive to the challenge of the moment.

Those who wander in a wilderness of uncertainty need reassurance that this experience, despite all appearances, is meaningful and formative. The journey towards recovery of lost meaning, or the resolution of a question, or finding that place where life is fruitful and we feel we belong, is long and testing. Change and growth take place by process. Pilgrims through a barren land need support in recognizing and then remembering the pillar-of-fire moments when the purpose of the journey and the presence of the guide became clear. The in-between times have their significance too; they are more than interruption. Here we come to know our own hearts; and also the heart of God.

The experience of meeting and separation within our relationship with God can be deeply unsettling, but a gift to us all the same. Restlessness and dissatisfaction may prove more positive than negative, directing us towards where our life lies in God. The felt absence of God may be down to someone's exhaustion or it may be a symptom of being drawn into a deeper intimacy with God through the calling forth of a more generous self-gift. The wise listener looks at what else is happening in this person's life: are their actions and attitudes developing creatively or destructively? Is the desire for God deepening or withering away? Are they trying too hard, believing everything rests on their effort, and nothing on God's gift? What does this person need: to rest physically, to let go of their belief that it's all down to them, or more actively to seek God's presence in prayer?

Such work of discernment is aided by the insights of the *Spiritual Exercises*. Those who accompany others help those they guide to pay attention to their feelings, desires and patterns of behaviour – comfortable and uncomfortable. They seek to be a balance at equilibrium, pushing the person neither this way nor that. Together they listen for the movement of the Spirit and the

disruptive impact of 'the enemy of our human progress.' As directors they know the only direction that matters is the direction
proposed by the Spirit of God; their words only serve to enable
the ones they guide to listen and to respond.

Growing in faith, hope and love

The life of the Spirit, characterized in the qualities of faith, hope
and love, is a very specific response to the experience of suffering.
Faith proposes that despite all appearances there is one alongside us in whom we can trust. Hope affirms that this unpromising
place is where God continues to create being and goodness. Love
is the willingness to go on offering what one has and is, and the
refusal to allow ourselves to become self-absorbed, aggressive and
fearful in the face of evil. As we have seen, what confuses us is
that we assume faith, hope and love to be feelings we enjoy when,
first and foremost, they are choices we make and ways we align
our lives. They are sails we set for the wind of the Spirit to fill, for
they have no lasting life except for this gift. When we are brought
low by difficulty and pain our natural optimism and strength can
ebb away; we do not feel trusting, hopeful or loving. Then we
need a guide to encourage us to act what we do not feel, unfurling
the sails once more, trusting in the power of the wind to move us
across the deep, wide sea.

It may be that neither the one who struggles nor the one who
seeks to support them can, for this moment, see very far in the
dark. But presence is often enough to give the courage necessary to
stay with the night until its hidden colours break forth in beauty.

A Cloud of Witnesses

Here are some brief biographical notes on the key witnesses whose testimony I have drawn on within this book. Needless to say, there are many others who also deserve a place, were there room.

George Eliot 1819–1880

George Eliot was the pen name of Mary Anne Evans, whose novels include *Middlemarch*, *The Mill on the Floss*, *Adam Bede*, *Daniel Deronda*, and the one referred to in this book, *Silas Marner: The Weaver of Raveloe*. Mary Anne, or as she later styled herself, Marian, was born in rural Warwickshire, a setting she returned to in many of her novels. Her personal life was the subject of gossip. She lived with a married man, George Lewes, for many years, and after his death went on to marry John Cross, 20 years her junior – not easy ground in Victorian England. Her religious journey was equally controversial. Brought up as a middle-of-the-road Anglican, Marian was influenced by her teacher to move towards a demanding evangelical expression of Christianity, akin to that followed by Silas Marner before his expulsion from his church. In time, Marian's reading led her to embrace the findings of a new age of scientific exploration that by their nature challenged the authority of the ecclesiastical establishment. She began to move away from mainstream Christianity, going on to translate *Das Leben Jesu* by David Strauss, an influential work that cast doubt on the divinity of Christ. Yet at the heart of much of her writing is the personal spiritual journey of ordinary people: their enduring quest to live generously and with integrity, in a way that contributed to the wellbeing of humanity. This search was a constant within Marian's life, with all its different expressions. In rejecting what she saw as the narrowness of some religious thinking she continued to express her vision of the spiritual dimension of all human existence.

Hadewijch

Hadewijch was a spiritual guide and poet who lived in the Rhineland in the thirteenth century. Within her surviving writings we have letters, poems and a series of visions, and these provide the bare bones of what we know about her. She was a Beguine – a member of a lay, female Christian community devoted to contemplative prayer and the service of the poor. In her early days she had rich experience of God, but as time went on she increasingly felt God's absence. At some point she was expelled from her community, perhaps accused of heresy. It is not easy to disentangle the experience of Hadewijch from the literary conventions of courtly love that she used to express her thought. To what degree does the poetic imagery she employs of the pained lover, whose devotion to his beloved is unrequited, reflect her own feelings? But in her letters in particular, we see the human person who mourns the friends she has lost and the familiar contact with God that is no longer hers. The vividness of her language, the drama of her visions, and the intensity of her desire to seek God whatever the cost can be daunting. However, she reaches across time with her insight that suffering is an inevitable part of our human existence and our spiritual growth. She assures us that whatever the season and whatever we might feel, 'Love' is always the true name and activity of God.

George Herbert, 1593–1633

George Herbert came from a wealthy and artistic family. He served for a time as University Orator in Trinity College, Cambridge and seemed set for life as a courtier. However, on the death of James 1, he sought ordination instead. He served as priest of the

parish of Bemerton and Fugglestone in Wiltshire and was generous in the care he gave his parishioners. His life as a priest, and
the work of the physical restoration of the parish church, found a
home within his poetry; but so did his recurrent ill-health, and his
struggles to reconcile his different desires and ambitions. Many
of his poems have been set to music as hymns, including *King
of Glory, King of Peace, Let All the World in Every Corner Sing*
and *Teach Me, My God and King*. What is evident in reading his
poetry is the intimacy and honesty of his relationship with God,
expressing joy, pain, doubt and deep faith in equal measure. In a
note written shortly before his death he entrusted his writings to
his friend, Nicholas Ferrar, describing it as, 'A picture of the many
spiritual conflicts that have passed betwixt God and my soul,
before I could subject mine to the will of Jesus my master; in
whose service I have now found perfect freedom.' He asked his
friend to read his work and then if he thought it might 'turn to the
advantage of any dejected soul', to publish it; but if not, he advised:
'let him burn it.' Fortunately, Nicholas Ferrar saw its worth!

Etty (Esther) Hillesum, 1914–1943

Etty Hillesum was from a Dutch Jewish family. After leaving
school she studied law and languages at university in Amsterdam,
making a living as a housekeeper and by giving private lessons in
Russian. Etty was intelligent, outgoing and inquisitive. She felt
she could be all over the place at times, lacking self-discipline and
depth. Her diary opens with her describing the gap between the
outwardly social and confident young woman her friends knew
and the inwardly tortured and muddled person she sometimes
felt herself to be. Helped by a psychotherapist friend she began a
spiritual search, spending regular time in meditation. She began
to keep a diary, through which she expressed the ups and downs
of her relationships, her quest for a more centred life and, increasingly, her reliance on God.

With the Nazi occupation of Holland, Etty's daily life became
subject to more and more restrictions. She refused to go into hiding,

not wishing to abandon her fellow Jews, and preferring to stay with the truth she had come to: that life remains rich and beautiful if only you remain open to receive it as it is. Eventually she was moved to a transit camp for Jews in Eastern Holland from where she continued to write letters to her friends. Finally she was transferred to Auschwitz, where she died in November 1943. Her letters and diaries survived in the hands of friends and were eventually published. What is striking in reading them is how as her outer life became more restricted, her inner self expanded, enabling her to face the reality of the suffering within and around her and still find life meaningful.

Gerard Manley Hopkins, 1844–1889

Hopkins became a Catholic in his early twenties and then sought ordination as a priest within the Jesuit order. From his youth he loved the natural world, keenly observing what he saw and expressing this in poetry and drawing. His poetry is quirky and original, reflecting his sense of humour, capacity for wonder and love for language. None of Hopkins' poetry was published in his lifetime. His major poem *The Wreck of the Deutschland* was turned down by the Jesuit periodical he hoped might publish it because of its unorthodox style and complexity. Nevertheless he continued to see his poetry, like his priesthood, as a servant of the sacramental nature of reality, hiding yet revealing the presence of Christ in all things created. From time to time he suffered from depression and much of the poetry explored in this book was written within times of immense personal struggle. Yet God is no less incarnate in these pained words than in the exuberant poetry of earlier days. He died of typhoid at the age of 44. His poetry was later published by his long-time friend and correspondent, Robert Bridges.

Ignatius of Loyola (Inigo Lopez de Loyola), 1491–1556

Ignatius was born in the Basque country at the castle of Loyola in the Kingdom of Navarre. As a young man he entered into a life of service at court, and took active part in a number of local wars. At the age of 30 his life changed when he was seriously injured by a cannonball in one such conflict at Pamplona. During a long convalescence, a bored Ignatius read books about the life of Christ and the saints, and found himself increasingly drawn to follow their example. In time Ignatius and his companions went on to found the Society of Jesus. But the road between his life-changing injury and this step was a long and meandering one involving a great deal of painful self-discovery. *The Spiritual Exercises* flow out of this slow journey into inner freedom. His own experience had shown the importance of discernment for anyone seeking to follow Christ. Not every impulse or desire can be trusted; nevertheless they have much to tell us about who we are and what ordinarily moves us. Just as taking a walk or running are physical exercises, Ignatius concerns himself with 'spiritual exercises' – those activities that enable us to be centred in God and in our truest, best selves. This also involves learning to distinguish thoughts and impulses that come from God (and therefore lead to life) from those that are destructive of self or other people.

The Spiritual Exercises takes the form of guidelines for someone leading another through a structured series of meditations aimed at achieving greater spiritual freedom. As such it is not a book to read, but to experience. Retreats on this basis are still offered, sometimes called 'individually guided' or 'Ignatian' retreats.

John of the Cross 1542–1591

Juan de Yepes was born in Fontiveros, a small village on the Castilian plains in Spain. His father, a silk merchant, died when he was a young boy, and poverty drove his mother to move with her children to the town of Medina del Campo. Here John received an education at a Jesuit school for orphans. In his teens he worked in a hospital caring for people with terminal illnesses. He became a Carmelite friar, embracing a way of life centred on contemplative prayer. With Teresa of Avila he set about the reform of the Carmelite order but met severe opposition, including a long period of imprisonment. From this prison experience, John wrote poetry, celebrating the love of God and how we meet God in experiences of 'night'. In his work as a spiritual guide John later wrote commentaries on his poetry, seeking to help make sense of the bewildering experience of being in a transforming relationship with God who is intimately close to us, but always beyond our grasp. His main works are: *The Ascent of Mount Carmel*, *The Dark Night*, *The Spiritual Canticle* and *The Living Flame of Love*. His poems and letters of spiritual guidance also survive. John's letters reveal him as a compassionate and encouraging spiritual guide, rather than the daunting and severe figure we might expect on first approaching his prose works.

Julian of Norwich, born around 1342

Julian was an 'anchoress' – a woman who chose a life of solitary prayer in a hermitage attached to the church of St. Julian in Norwich. The life of an anchorite might seem strange and extreme to us, but it was an accepted and valued role in her time. In her solitude, Julian not only sought God, but acted as a spiritual guide for others. Her role as an intercessor was important too, supporting both living and dead on their journey to God.

The anchoress' cell was a small stone dwelling with one or more rooms attached to a church, often with a garden. The anchoress usually had a maid to look after her practical needs. Norwich was a major city and port in medieval times and Julian's cell would have been in the heart of the community rather than in a remote place. We know little about Julian's life; we do not even know her true name as by tradition an anchoress was given the name of the church she was attached to. She describes how in her thirty-first year she had a serious illness; in her near-death state she received a number of visions of the Crucified Christ. On her recovery she pondered the meaning of what she had experienced and wrote down her reflections; a first version, close to the time of her experience, and a second and fuller version some 15 to 20 years later. This work was written in English, rather than in the Latin more usual for spiritual works of the time, as Julian wanted it to be of benefit to all her 'fellow Christians' and not just clergy and religious. Julian's theology flows from the realities of life as reflected on through prayer. She comes across as a well-grounded, compassionate and wise person – someone you would feel safe in talking to and count on for good advice.

Thérèse of Lisieux 1873–1897

Thérèse Martin began writing her spiritual autobiography, later published as *Story of a Soul*, some two years before her death from tuberculosis. In it she describes the path by which she came to join the Carmelite community at Lisieux at the age of 15, the twists and turns of her own faith journey and the spiritual crisis that afflicted her in her latter years. After her death, *Story of a Soul* proved hugely popular. She was canonized in 1925 when – if still alive – she would have only been in her early fifties. To a modern reader Thérèse's writings may seem rather sentimental; but her crisis of faith was all too real. She had to work her way through a prolonged darkness where any sense of intimacy with God was lost to her. Even though she was able to weave this sense of estrangement from God into her own soul story, she still missed this closeness dreadfully.

Simone Weil, 1909–1943

Simone Weil was born in Paris to non-observant Jewish parents. From her early days she had a strong sense of justice, and compassion for those who were suffering. She was a brilliant philosopher and writer, with a breadth of interest in social and political movements and in the insights of different faith traditions. Though her main occupation was as a teacher she took leave of absence to work in factories and in the fields to gain understanding of the oppression of those who worked long hours for little pay. She was active in the union movement and was also briefly involved in the Spanish Civil War on the Republican side. In her late twenties she had a series of religious experiences that drew her towards Christianity, though she resisted being baptized as she felt there was truth to be found in all faiths. She had always struggled with ill health, and she died in Ashford, Kent in 1943 from tuberculosis, refusing to eat more food than she believed people in occupied France had available to them.

Most of her writing was published after her death. These include *The Need for Roots*, *Gravity and Grace*, *On Science, Necessity and the Love of God*, and *Waiting for God*, the source drawn on for this book. She believed that the experience of affliction (*malheur*) leads us most deeply into God through Christ. The cross is a place where separation is felt but meeting takes place.

William Williams, 1717–1791

Williams was born in Cefn-y-Coed near Llandovery, where his father, a farmer, was an elder in the Cefnarthen Independent Church. Williams' life was turned around at the age of 20 on hearing a sermon given by the Methodist preacher, Howell Harris, in Talgarth churchyard. He became a deacon in the Anglican Church, but his growing involvement in the Methodist revival meant he was never ordained as a priest. He travelled widely through Wales, preaching and teaching – often in the open air – and establishing new Methodist fellowships. Like the Wesley brothers, he saw hymn writing as a means of telling the Gospel story and of expressing in song the quality of faith that brings about inner transformation. He wrote in Welsh, the language accessible for the people he lived and worked among. Besides hymn writing Williams also wrote poetry and prose as resources for the journeys of those he ministered to. Williams is popularly known as the sweet songster of Wales because of the rich heritage of his hymns.